D1418296

Extraordinary Jobs in

SPORTS

Also in the Extraordinary Jobs series:

Extraordinary Jobs in

SPORTS

ALECIA T. DEVANTIER & CAROL A. TURKINGTON

Ferguson

An imprint of Infobase Publishing

Extraordinary Jobs in Sports

Ferguson
An imprint of Infobase Publishing
132 West 31st Street
New York NY 10001

Library of Congress Cataloging-in-Publication Data

Devantier, Alecia T.
  Extraordinary jobs in sports / Alecia T. Devantier and Carol A. Turkington.
    p. cm.
  Includes index.
  ISBN 0-8160-5861-X (alk. paper)
1. Sports—Vocational guidance. I. Turkington, Carol. II. Title.
  GV734.3 D48 2006
  796.023—dc 22   2006008417

Ferguson books are available at special discounts when purchased in bulk quantities for businesses, associations, institutions, or sales promotions. Please call our Special Sales Department in New York at (212) 967-8800 or (800) 322-8755.

You can find Ferguson on the World Wide Web at http://www.fergpubco.com

Text design by Mary Susan Ryan-Flynn
Cover design by Salvatore Luongo

Printed in the United States of America

VB MSRF 10 9 8 7 6 5 4 3 2 1

This book is printed on acid-free paper.

CONTENTS

ACKNOWLEDGMENTS

This book wouldn't have been possible without the help of countless others who referred us to individuals to interview and came up with information about a wide variety of odd and unusual jobs. We deeply appreciate the time and generosity of all those individuals who took the time to talk to us about their unusual jobs in sports. Thanks also to all the people who helped with interviews and information and the production of this book, including Michael McGovern, Susan Shelly McGovern, and Don Stewart. Thanks also to our editors James Chambers and Sarah Fogarty, to Vanessa Nittoli, to our agents Ed Claflin of Ed Claflin Literary Associates and Gene Brissie of James Peter Associates, and to Michael and Kara.

ARE YOU CUT OUT FOR A SPORTS CAREER?

Do you dream of careening over the ice in a Zamboni, or flying down a drag strip in a Funny Car? Does your heart beat faster when you're flying over ten-foot Grand Prix jumps on a thoroughbred hunter? Perhaps you can't imagine anything better than sinking a perfect putt or the satisfying *thwack* of a puck slamming into the net.

If you want a sports career, realize right now that it takes talent, sweat, hard work, and lots of luck to succeed. Take some time to think about the kind of person you are and the sorts of experiences you dream of having. Ask yourself: *Am I passionate about this sport?* Remember, most of these jobs don't pay much when you first start out. Sure, there are stars who bring home seven-figure checks, but there are plenty of others who never reach those dizzying heights. Are you in it for the money, the glory, or the love of the game?

Yet no matter what position you play or what level you reach, a career in sports does offer something that's much harder to measure—the satisfaction of doing what you love. You can't put a price on that.

Of course, loving what you do is only part of having a successful sports career. You've also got to be good at what you want to do. Most sports jobs require real talent, and if you're going to go after one of them, you need to be really good at it. Whether you're thinking of becoming a tennis pro, a hockey player, a sports photographer, or team manager, you need to have the talent to do that job better than most other people. You also have to be willing to work hard. Many jobs in the sports world don't fit into the traditional 9-to-5 workday. Are you willing to work at night, on the weekends, or during particular seasons?

The sports industry is a booming field, accounting for more than 5 million jobs and many millions of dollars in annual revenues. The NBA, NFL, MLB, NASCAR, and major league soccer continue to expand, along with sports-related ventures by corporate giants such as NBC Sports, Disney, Warner, and Fox Sports—meaning job opportunities are increasing daily. You can find lucrative job opportunities in the sports industry at all levels, including internships, entry level, management, and executive-level positions in the following fields:

- Administration and management
- Broadcasting
- Computers and graphic design
- Corporate sponsors
- Health and fitness
- Print media
- Professional sports
- Professional teams and leagues
- Public relations and advertising
- Radio and TV
- Recreation and leisure
- Sporting events and promotions
- Sporting goods
- Sports information
- Sports marketing and sales

Although there are plenty of opportunities, you've still got to be willing to work hard. Too many times, kids have the idea that they'll graduate into a world of sports with people just dying to give them a job. It can be unbelievably hard to get started in this business. Of course, a lucky few are born into sports families, where Mom or Dad or Aunt Sara already works in the business. If your dad is already a world-class drag racer, you've got it made if you want to follow in his footsteps. If your mom is already an ace tennis pro or a team manager—well, you've probably got a big head start. But for the rest of you—it can be a long, hard slog to the top.

Everybody knows about the typical jobs in sports. We wrote this book to help you see the world of unusual careers you may never have thought about—jobs you may not have known existed, or that you didn't realize paid a decent salary. Once you see the possibilities, start dreaming about how to reach them. Remember, if you've got a dream, you owe it to yourself to go after it, no matter how unusual, difficult, or just plain batty it may seem to others.

You'll need to realize that there may be other people who aren't so happy with your career choice. You may hear complaints from your family and friends who just can't understand why you don't want a "regular" job. Some people think working in sports only qualifies as a hobby—something you do until a "real" job comes along. Sure, you can play ice hockey, kick around a soccer ball, bat a few runs home with the gals after work. But nobody really makes a living like that! Can you imagine what Hank Aaron's mom said when he told her he wanted to spend the rest of his life making a living playing baseball?

Have you inherited a lot of *shoulds* in thinking about the kind of person you want to be? These *shoulds* inside your head can be a major stumbling block in finding and enjoying a sports career. If you confide your career dreams to some of these people, you may find they try to discourage you. Can you handle their continuous skepticism?

If you decide to seek out a career in the sports field, you'll almost certainly encounter setbacks. How do you handle adversity? How do you feel when you fail? If you can pick yourself up and keep going, you've probably got the temperament to survive the rocky road to a sports career.

What's become clear as we researched this book is that a career in sports is more than a job—it's a way of looking at life, with gusto and verve. Living and working in the world of sports isn't necessarily an easy career. But if you allow yourself to explore the options that are out there, you'll find that work and play often tend to become the same thing. So push past your doubts and fears—and let your journey begin!

Carol A. Turkington
Alecia T. Devantier

HOW TO USE THIS BOOK

Students face a lot of pressure to decide what they want to be when they grow up. If you're not interested in a traditional 9-to-5 job—if you're an adventurous spirit looking for a unique way to make a living, where can you go to find out answers you might have about these exciting, nontraditional jobs?

Where can you go to find out how to become a Grand Prix dressage rider, traveling the horse show circuit? What does it take to become a hockey player or a golf ball diver? Where do you learn how to be a tennis pro? Is it really possible to make a living as a sports team mascot? Where would you go for training if you want to be a minor league team manager or a pit crew member? What's the job outlook for team physicians?

Look no further. From athletic director to Zamboni driver, this book takes you inside the world of a number of different sports-related jobs, answering questions you might have, letting you know what to expect if you pursue that career, introducing you to someone making a living that way, and providing resources if you want to do further research.

THE JOB PROFILES

All job profiles in this book have been broken down into the following fact-filled sections: At a Glance, Overview, and Interview. Each offers a distinct perspective on the job, and taken together give you a full view of the job in question.

At a Glance

Each entry starts out with an *At a Glance* box, offering a snapshot of important basic information to give you a quick glimpse of that particular job, including salary, education, requirements, personal attributes, and outlook.

✓ *Salary range.* What can you expect to make? Salary ranges for the jobs in this book are as accurate as possible; many are based on the U.S. Bureau of Labor Statistics' *Occupational Outlook Handbook*. Information also comes from individuals, actual job ads, employers, and experts in that field. It's important to remember that salaries for any particular job vary greatly depending on experience, geographic location, and level of education.

✓ *Education/Experience.* What kind of education or experience does the job require? This section will give you some information about the types of education or experience requirements the job might call for.

✓ *Personal attributes.* Do you have what it takes to do this job? How do you think of yourself? How would someone else describe you? This section will give you an idea of some of the personality characteristics and traits that might be useful to you if you choose this career. These attributes were collected from articles written about the job, as well as recommendations from employers and people actually doing the jobs, working in the field.

✓ *Requirements.* Are you qualified? You might as well make sure you meet any health, medical, or screening requirements before going any further with your job pursuit.

✓ *Outlook.* What are your chances of finding a job in the sports business?

This section is based in part on the *Occupational Outlook Handbook,* as well as on interviews with employers and experts. This information is typically a "best guess" based on the information that's available right now, including changes in the economy, situations in the United States and around the world, job trends, and retirement levels. These and many other factors can influence changes in the availability of jobs in sports.

Overview

This section will give you an idea of what to expect from the job. For most of these unusual jobs, there really is no such thing as an average day. Each day is a whole new adventure, bringing with it a unique set of challenges and rewards. This section will give you an idea of what a person in this position might expect on a day-to-day basis.

The overview also gives you more details about how to get into the profession, offering a more detailed look at the required training or education, if needed, and providing an in-depth look at what to expect during that training or educational period.

No job is perfect, and **Pitfalls** takes a look at some of the obvious and maybe not-so-obvious problems with the job. Don't let the pitfalls discourage you from pursuing a career; they are just things to be aware of while making your decision.

For many people, loving their job so much that they look forward to going to work every day is enough of a perk. **Perks** looks at some of the other benefits of the job you may not have considered.

What can you do now to start working toward the career of your dreams? **Get a Jump on the Job** will give you some ideas and suggestions for things that you can do now, even before graduating, to start preparing for this job. Opportunities include training programs, internships, groups and organizations to join, as well as practical skills to learn.

Interview

In addition to taking a general look at the job, each entry features a discussion with someone who is lucky enough to do this job for a living. In addition to giving you an inside look at the job, this interview provides valuable tips for anyone interested in pursuing a career in the same field.

APPENDIXES

Appendix A (Associations, Organizations, and Web Sites) lists places to look for additional information about each specific job, including professional associations, societies, unions, training programs, forums, and periodicals. Associations and other groups are a great source of information, and there's an association for just about every job you can imagine. Many groups and associations have a student membership level, which you can join by paying a small fee. There are many advantages to joining an association, including the chance to make important contacts, receive helpful newsletters, and attend workshops or conferences. Some associations also offer scholarships that will make it easier to further your education.

In **Appendix B (Online Career Resources)** we've gathered some of the best general Web sites about unusual jobs in the sports industry, along with a host of very specific Web sites tailored to individual sports-related jobs. Use these as a springboard to your own Internet research. Of course, all of this information is current as we've written this book, but Web site addresses do change. If you can't find what you're looking for at a given address, do a simple Internet search. The page may have been moved to a different location.

READ MORE ABOUT IT

In this back-of-the-book listing, we've gathered some helpful books that can give you more detailed information about each job we discuss in this book. Find these at the library or bookstore if you want to learn even more about jobs in the sports world.

ATHLETIC DIRECTOR, HIGH SCHOOL

OVERVIEW

The job of a high school athletic director means having to wear many hats. You have to be part administrator, part organizer, part mediator, part fund-raiser, and all business. Which is not to suggest that the job isn't an enjoyable way to make a living, because it can be. If you love sports and working with kids, and see your athletic program as an extension of a student's education, being an athletic director can be an enormously rewarding occupation. Just be prepared to work hard and long.

An athletic director organizes and administers a school district's overall physical education program, which includes high school, junior high, and intramural teams. In a large district, that could mean overseeing nearly 50 different teams. Some athletic directors are also in charge of community programs that use school district facilities.

The athletic director has to play a role in evaluating, hiring, and firing coaches; facilitate transportation needs; keep tabs on student-athletes to make sure they are academically eligible; prepare and implement the interscholastic and community recreation budgets; order equipment; supervise ticket sales and fund-raising events; coordinate facility use, making sure every team that needs a field or a gym for practice or games has one; oversee athletes' physical examinations and the insurance program covering high school

athletics; plan and supervise recognition programs for athletes; serve on the school board's extracurricular committee; report to the school board and the high school administrators; attend meetings of district and state committees; and foster positive

Steve Polonus, athletic director

Steve Polonus is the athletic director at Wilson High School, a large suburban school outside Reading, Pennsylvania, slightly more than an hour northwest of Philadelphia. He estimates that during an average week, he spends at least nine hours watching games involving Wilson teams. "People who only see me at this event or that event ... maybe they think that's all I do during the week, watch games," says Polonus, laughing. "But they don't realize that my day starts before 8 every morning."

And those days often last into the evening and extend to many Saturdays. Regular hours are not part of the territory of a high school athletic director. Polonus oversees, organizes, and administers 26 varsity interscholastic teams, 22 junior high interscholastic teams, intramural, and community recreation programs.

"I think the job has changed a lot over the last 10 years," Polonus says. "Just look at how youth sports have changed over the last decade; that's blown this job up. Ten years ago, you would've had a tough time finding an athletic director that didn't teach a couple of classes. Now, you'd have a tough time finding one that does. Sports have been added; policies, rules and regulations have increased; media coverage has increased; and parents' involvement has increased. All those things have added hours to the workload."

Polonus had been a teacher and coach at McCaskey High School in Lancaster, Pennsylvania, when he felt it was time "to do something different." That something turned out to be the athletic director's job at McCaskey.

But Polonus' education—an undergraduate degree from Elizabethtown College and a master's degree from Eastern College—had been in business administration, business education, and accounting. So when he made the decision to move into the athletic director's office, he went to West Chester University and earned a master's degree in Athletic Administration.

"I enjoyed the educational part of it [at West Chester], and I enjoyed working with high school kids and coaches," he says. "I knew it took a special kind of person to be a high school coach; it's tough to be a good father, a good husband, and a good coach. But this job, even though there are a lot of hours, they're not concentrated like a coach's during the season. There's rarely a day that goes by that I don't see my kids. Coaching a season is a whole different thing, but being an athletic director has made my family life more manageable."

relations between their and other schools as well as with the community.

Athletic directors are expected to attend as many of their school's games as possible. Sometimes they go to show support for their athletes and coaches. Other times they serve as the game manager for that particular contest, which means it's up to them to keep control of the crowd and hand out discipline if students get a bit out of control. All games are either right after school or in the evenings. With many schools opening at 8 a.m., and with evening games beginning at 6:30, athletic directors may not get home until 10 p.m., or later if the game is on the road. Many high schools also schedule events on Saturdays, which makes for a six-day week with very little time to relax.

Now comes what most athletic directors regard as the most difficult part of the job: dealing with unhappy parents. The pressure for students to excel in high

Polonus may not be the coach of a team, but he still considers himself to be a coach. "I view my coaches as my team," he says. "My team is my coaches, and my coaches are my 'players.' I help train them and then I put them out there on the field and let them go with it. I still view myself as a coach, only now with adults, professional people."

"One of the things I like to do is help people, and I would say 75 percent of my time is spent interacting with people, supporting them, helping them. If you go into education it's likely that you are going to be a helpful kind of person."

The worst part of the job for Polonus are those times when "negative action" has to be taken to discipline his coaches, and when he has to mediate disputes between disgruntled parents and coaches.

But what he tries to do is hire the best people he can, set a tone and a standard of excellence, and then "step back and watch those people go to work."

"I think coaches look to me for direction," Polonus says. "But if you hire good people, you don't have to be looking over their shoulder all the time. You can turn them loose and let them run."

The key to running a successful athletic department, Polonus says, is organization, attention to detail, and putting systems in place that can sustain themselves year after year.

"Once you have those systems in place," Polonus says, "things can sort of take care of themselves."

Which is not to say, even if all systems are go, that there isn't a lot to think about.

"My guess is that I probably have 300 details a day to care of," he says. "If you're not detail-oriented and you miss one of those 300 details, everyone is going to know. If one out of every 100 buses doesn't get where it's supposed to be, that's not good. If you allow an [academically] ineligible kid to play for the football team, that's not good.

"High school sports have become pretty high profile, so most mistakes you make will not go unnoticed."

If you're thinking that you might like to become an athletic director, Polonus suggests teaching and coaching first. "Teaching will give you a strong educational background," he says. "And by coaching you'll understand what it takes to be a coach."

That combination should put you well on your way to the athletic director's chair.

school sports has increased considerably over the last decade. Many parents think their child is going to turn into the next Michael Jordan, Tiger Woods, or Michelle Wie. And for that next Michael, Tiger, or Michelle to realize his or her potential, it's absolutely necessary that they earn a college scholarship—or so the parents think.

But sometimes parents overestimate the ability of their children. When high school coaches don't play these students as much as their parents want, or when they play them in positions other than their parents want, the parents are not happy campers. It's not unusual for these disputes to end up in the athletic director's office. It can be very uncomfortable, but unfortunately, that's part of the territory.

As an athletic director, you will provide guidance and leadership to your coaches, develop a sense of pride and spirit in your school, and watch as a group of motivated, talented athletes enjoy some of the best years of their lives.

You also get the chance to shape an athletic program according to your ideals and priorities. In a perfect world, that would mean making sure your school's athletic program provides an educational component, teaching student-athletes on-the-field life lessons that they can't learn in the classroom.

Pitfalls

The job entails long hours, nights, and weekends. There is also a lot of scheduling and detail work, so it's important that you have expert organizational skills. Meetings with upset parents are another regular challenge.

Perks

You get to set the tone for your school's athletic department. Sports can be an important part of a school, because of the spirit they provide and the sense of community they foster. Being responsible, in many ways, for a successful athletic program can be an invaluable experience.

Get a Jump on the Job

Try to get as much background as you can as a teacher, a coach, and an administrator. Being an athletic director involves components of all three disciplines.

BOXER

OVERVIEW

With the exception of its declining popularity, boxing hasn't changed much since its heyday of the 1930s and '40s. Compared to professional boxing, amateur boxing is still a largely unregulated profession in which managers and promoters routinely take advantage of boxers. Yet it remains an attractive avenue for many: Due to its one-on-one nature, boxing is a sport where the underdog seemingly has a chance. One well-timed punch is all it takes to change a boxer's life.

Boxing rewards talented fighters with fame and fortune. And because it has weight classes ranging from 105 pounds (strawweight) to unlimited (heavyweight), athletes of virtually any size can compete.

Still, the road to the top is a long one in this trade. Many fighters work for several years, sometimes well over a decade, before getting a shot at a big payday. Most boxers start out in the amateur league at a gym or YMCA in their preteen years, where they learn the basics of boxing. Then, as teenagers and young men, they compete at high-profile amateur tournaments such as the Golden Gloves.

The goal of almost any amateur boxer is to earn a spot on the U.S. Olympic team, which almost always results in a promotional contract for your first professional bout. However, only 11 boxers make the U.S. team every four years. Most of those left behind have to wrangle impressive wins in at least 10 pro fights before a promoter will take a chance on signing them. Although promoters are often criticized for hurting boxing, they remain essential to building a career in the sport's current

AT A GLANCE (continued)

be in the ring. If a fighter is knocked out, most states automatically suspend that fighter for 30 days. If a state suspends a boxer for any reason, other state commissions are obliged to honor that suspension.

Outlook

Once considered one of the two most popular sports in America, boxing has slowly declined into second-tier status over the past 50 years, because of numerous incidents (such as Mike Tyson biting off Evander Holyfield's ear in 1997). However, 2005 showed that the sport still has plenty of life left in it. The first half of the year was packed with memorable fights, such as the Diego Corrales–Jose Luis Castillo lightweight slugfest. A February welterweight title bout in St. Louis set an indoor attendance record, broken in May by a junior welterweight title fight in Manchester, England. Meanwhile, movies such as *Million Dollar Baby* and *Cinderella Man* and the reality TV show *The Contender* attracted new fans. While fighters might not have the opportunity to earn the notoriety they could have enjoyed 50 years ago, the sport certainly has a future, especially among certain niche audiences.

organizational structure. A good promoter will get you reputable opponents. More importantly, he'll get you on TV and out in front of the fans.

Early in your career, you'll likely be fighting for a few hundred dollars per bout as your manager tries to build your record and experience in hopes of attracting a promoter. You'll have to stay in training almost constantly during this period, as your fight schedule will be unpredictable. Bouts can be arranged, only to fall through for a variety of reasons, such as an injury of a would-be opponent. Your manager could then find you a fight on short notice.

As your record and reputation improve, your purses should slowly increase. Once you're working with a promoter, you'll fight less often against better opposition. This will give you a more stable training schedule and more time to prepare for an opponent.

Patience, perseverance, and having a trustworthy manager are key in overcoming the difficulties that face almost any fighter.

Pitfalls

While boxing might look glamorous on television, it can be a difficult trade. You're likely to endure bumps and bruises along the way, both in and out of the ring. You might lose a decision you thought you'd earned. Your manager or promoter might try to cheat you out of money. Pay for boxers who haven't yet reached world-class status is miniscule, and fights can be infrequent due to forces beyond a fighter's control. Once you're earning big purses, your trainer, manager, and promoter will receive a percentage of the money. Since boxing is such a demanding sport, you'll have to be prepared to work out as often as three times a day before a fight. Non-heavyweight fighters must weigh below a certain limit before each fight, so you'll have to be strict with your diet.

Perks

Like any athlete, boxers have the chance to become stars. With that comes all the things the go hand-in-hand with stardom, such as money, media attention, and endorsements. Most fighters are driven by the dream of winning a world title and earning the respect that comes with being a champion.

Get a Jump on the Job

Finding out if you have what it takes to get in the ring is as simple as locating a

Keenan Collins, boxer

Keenan Collins was a 24-year-old ex-felon playing semi-pro basketball in Pottsville, Pennsylvania, back in early 2001. Wanting to stay in shape, he checked out King's Boxing Gym in Reading, Pennsylvania, where he was living at a halfway house.

Collins hasn't played basketball since.

Although he got a late start in boxing, he took his time in completing a 25-bout amateur career. The lanky Collins, who competes at 147 pounds, won 21 of those fights, with each of his four defeats owed to nationally ranked opponents. He turned pro in May 2004 at the age of 27. In Collins' first pro bout, he faced an opponent who was 3-0. One punch from Collins in the second round knocked his opponent out cold. He went on to win three more fights that year, all by knockout. One of those bouts came on just six hours' notice.

In December 2004, he faced unbeaten prospect Mike Torres in Atlantic City in a fight preceding an ESPN-televised main event. It was a great opportunity for Collins to get exposure. Although Collins lost the fight, he did make a career-high of $1,700 that night.

He started 2005 with three wins, traveling to North Carolina for two of those, but fights are hard to come by for Collins, whose record of 7-1 with seven knockouts made him a high risk–low reward opponent for most potential foes. Collins worked a full-time job during the day when he was fighting in the amateurs. Today, his managers Jeff Nigrelli and Marshall Kauffman pay Collins' bills from money they get from local sponsors so Collins can fully devote himself to boxing. Nigrelli and Kauffman are hoping to attract a major promoter for Collins.

"The stage I'm in now, I'm wanting to fight, not knowing when I'm gonna fight or if I'm gonna fight, thinking I'm gonna fight and not fighting, getting ready for a fight and still not fighting," Collins says. "As far as training, I like to train. After a fight, they say 'take a week off.' I can't take a week off. In three days, I'm shadow boxing, I want to fight. I like boxing."

A typical day for Collins begins at 5 a.m., when he gets up to do roadwork (long-distance jogging). He returns to his apartment above King's Gym to care for his young daughter, then goes downstairs to train from 2 p.m. to 4 p.m. After a short break, he's out running again by 5:30 p.m.

While growing up in York, Pennsylvania, Collins got caught up in the street life, dealing drugs and eventually serving three and a half years in state prison for aggravated assault. Although he hasn't gotten so much as a video store late fee since being released, he still carries the "killer instinct" he learned on the streets. "I like fighting," he says. "All my life I liked to fight. I don't know if that's something bad, but I get paid to do something that I like doing."

Still, Collins doesn't think a poor, troubled background is a prerequisite for a fighter. Strong physical skills, as well as a competitive nature and a willingness to fight, are the essential ingredients, he believes. Although Collins has dreams of world titles and the money that comes with them, he's realistic about his chances, aware that there will have to be life after boxing. After signing with a promoter and getting fights on a set basis, he plans to return to community college, where he'll work toward a degree in computer science.

"You don't need a college degree to throw a punch," he said. "But everyone can't box. There's only one champion. If you strive to be a doctor or a lawyer, there are millions of doctors and millions of lawyers. In boxing, there are only one or two guys that's 'the man.' So to be a boxer, you have to understand that not everyone is gonna be a millionaire. If you want to box because you want to box, that's good. If you want to box to make money, then you're in the wrong sport."

local boxing gym. If the trainer is willing to work with you, you should start out by learning the basics before competing in your first amateur fight. You'll learn quickly whether the sport is for you.

BOXING TRAINER

OVERVIEW

Boxing trainers have been glorified by fictional characters such as Mickey in *Rocky* and Frankie Dunn in *Million Dollar Baby*, but it takes a lot of work, and plenty of luck, before a trainer can walk a fighter to the ring on national television.

For starters, you need to learn the sport. The best way to do this is to actually box. You don't need to focus on becoming a professional fighter. Many successful trainers, such as HBO commentator Emanuel Steward, began training fighters after completing successful amateur careers. Learning the basics, and eventually the intricacies, of the sport will be essential down the road when you have to teach a raw talent to box.

Develop a reputation in the sport, and you'll have instant credibility when you decide to retire and become a trainer. Former world champion Buddy McGirt, who retired in 1997, was voted trainer of the year in 2002 for his work with Arturo Gatti. Freddie Roach, a featherweight contender in the early 1980s, was trainer of the year in 2003 and is in demand more than any trainer in the business.

Roach spent several years learning the trade as a protégé of legendary trainer Eddie Futch, who trained Roach during his pro boxing career (1978–86). Roach then served as an assistant to Futch for several years before slowly taking on his own fighters, beginning with light heavyweight champion Virgil Hill. This type of apprenticeship is common, and ideal, in the trade. Assistants are expected to do much of the grunt work for their busy boss, including holding the punch mitts, taping hands, and hugging the heavy bag.

When they make the leap from assistant to full-time trainers, most trainers open their own gym. Like starting a small business, this takes some start-up money—as much as $20,000—to obtain equipment and a building. Gyms come in all shapes and sizes. Trainer Marshall Kauffman built a small gym in the back of his furniture shop in downtown Reading, Pennsylvania. Other gyms, like the famed Gleason's Gym in Brooklyn, are much bigger and swankier than the typical boxing gym.

No matter where you decide to work, much of your success will depend upon the fighters you land. Emanuel Steward, for example, broke through in the mid-1970s when a young Thomas Hearns walked into his Kronk Gym in Detroit. Hearns blossomed into one of the most successful fighters of the 1980s, and Steward's reputation grew as a result. Nowadays, Stew-ard doesn't have to work with raw talent; established names seek him out.

Developing that kind of reputation is the goal of most trainers. Some, however, choose to keep things simple by sticking with a limited number of professionals. This helps their focus and often strengthens a one-on-one relationship with a fighter. They might also work with a number of young amateur fighters. Many trainers do this for free, with their desire to get kids off the street greater than their desire to make money. Typically, though, trainers charge amateur fighters a reasonable monthly fee, kind of like your local fitness club.

Whatever their situation, trainers must be experts in boxing skills and training techniques. You'll have to be ready to be tough on a fighter who isn't doing what you've asked. You'll also have to develop game plans to defeat opponents, which comes from knowing your fighter's and the opponent's strengths and weaknesses. It often takes trainers years of developing these skills on the job before being ready to handle world-class fighters.

Pitfalls

Boxers tend to switch trainers often, so a trainer's roster of fighters is often subject to change. Unless you're working in Las Vegas or Atlantic City, where most big fights are held, the job is sure to involve a lot of travel. Hours can get hectic, depending on the number of fighters you work with and the amount of attention they demand.

Perks

For most trainers, continued involvement in boxing long after their fighting days have passed is a major reason for getting into the profession. Each fighter with world-title aspirations presents a chance for a trainer

Marshall Kauffman, boxing trainer

After graduating from high school in 1981, Marshall Kauffman was a young man without direction. Slowly, boxing began to fill the void. He began showing up at a local gym run by his uncle, veteran trainer Rich Ormsbee, and quickly became passionate about the sport. He dropped 67 pounds, as requested by Ormsbee, in order to fight. Late at night, Ormsbee would walk into his gym thinking no one was around, only to find his nephew shadowboxing in front of a mirror.

By most accounts, Kauffman had a great deal of natural ability as a fighter, but he was selling drugs when he wasn't in the gym, and wound up serving nine months in prison. Behind bars, Kauffman found religion. After he was released, he started a small furniture business in Reading, Pennsylvania, fought his only pro bout in 1988, and began working part time as a trainer.

Hoping boxing could do for others what it helped do for him, Kauffman took up training full time. In 1995 he founded King's Gym. The name stands for "Kids In Need of Guidance." Ten years later, Kauffman admits he's still learning the craft. He believes a good trainer needs five to 10 years of experience before being ready to handle world-class fighters. "My downfall was I had nobody else to learn from," he says. "I had to pick it up on my own and I had to watch and observe. I didn't come in as an assistant to someone else. I learned a lot just by going to the Philly gyms and watching boxing and just having a passion for it."

Kauffman began working with local boys who came in off the street, eventually working with professionals. His first break of sorts came when junior middleweight Bobby Heath, a North Carolina native, began working out at King's Gym. Under Kauffman's direction, Heath worked his way into some nationally televised fights. He later worked with late world champion Steve Little toward the end of Little's career, and a handful of other fighters who served as trial horses (basically, an opponent with little chance of winning) for contenders. His big break came in 1999, when seven students from Thaddeus Stevens Tech in nearby Lancaster showed up at the gym wanting to start a boxing club.

Among them was a skinny 19-year-old named Kermit Cintron. Cintron's talent quickly became apparent, and soon Kauffman signed on as his trainer and co-manager. By the end of 2005, Cintron had brought unprecedented notoriety to Kauffman and his gym, running up a record of 24-1 with 22 KOs, fighting on HBO and ESPN pay-per-view, and earning a No. 6 world ranking at welterweight from boxing magazine *The Ring*. The biggest single payday Kauffman has had as a trainer—$50,000—came working Cintron's corner.

Kauffman's success with Cintron helped him attract talented amateurs Dat Nguyen and Chad Aquino, both of whom turned pro under Kauffman's guidance. Unbeaten junior middleweight contender Tarvis Simms moved to Reading in 2004 to train at King's. Local welterweight Keenan Collins found his way onto an ESPN-televised show in just his fifth pro fight. The attention also helped Kauffman land sponsorship for his son, Travis, an amateur super heavyweight rated No. 1 in the country at the end of 2005.

With his time increasingly devoted to training pros and his son, Kauffman admits that the original mission of his gym has suffered. In late 2005, he readjusted his schedule. Now, Kauffman typically runs his business from 7 a.m. to 2 p.m., trains his professional fighters from 2 to 4 p.m., then works with amateurs from 4 to 6:30 p.m. He's usually in the gym until at least 7, however, making

(continues)

(continued)

for a 12-hour day. "It's been hard to keep that as a focus," he says of working with kids. "I'm trying to make sure that I re-channel my thinking. That's why I stopped bringing Kermit and the pros in here when the amateurs are in here. A lot of times, I can't give them the attention when the pros are in here and they're all training at the same time. I felt like I was neglecting them, so I split it up so I could start to give them more attention again."

With so many fighters demanding his time, Kauffman has his eyes in several places at once during a typical training session. "Sometimes it goes smooth; sometimes it's screwy," he says. "There's personalities that get involved. Kermit might want more attention than Keenan, or Keenan might want more attention than Kermit. But for the most part, they've been good."

Although working with established talent can be rewarding, both personally and financially, Kauffman said his biggest thrill still comes from watching newcomers pick up the basics. "What I like best about it is seeing results," he says. "That's the best. It's like a carpenter or someone building a house and seeing the house built. That's what I like."

to get a piece of the limelight. And fighters who command six- and seven-figure payouts enable trainers to earn a very decent living, and maybe even strike it rich.

Get a Jump on the Job

The ideal way to learn the trade is to work as an assistant at a boxing gym. While it's possible to land these positions by simply showing up and offering your services, you typically have to know a trainer before he will take you on as an assistant. If you're hired, don't expect much in the way of pay. In other words, plan on keeping that day job.

BULL RIDER

OVERVIEW

Eight seconds may be a full day on the job for a bull rider, but it might seem more like an eternity for the rider himself, strapped to a 2,000-pound bull. For the fans in the stands, it's those eight seconds of heart-pounding excitement that makes bull riding one of rodeo's most popular events.

The object of bull riding is simple: You must stay on board for at least eight seconds. A flat braided rope is wrapped around the bull's chest; one end of the rope is threaded through a loop on the other end of the rope, and pulled tight. The rider holds onto the rope, wrapping it around one hand or weaving it through his fingers. With a nod of the head signaling the rider is ready, the chute opens and the bull rockets out of the gate.

That's when the clock starts. The bull rider must hold on with only one hand for eight seconds while the bull bucks, jumps, spins, or kicks, trying to get the rider off his back. If the rider's free hand touches himself or the bull, the rider is disqualified.

To protect themselves, all bull riders wear several pieces of protective clothing. Most important is a glove on their riding hand (the hand holding the rope), which helps prevent rope burn and makes it easier for the rider to hang onto the rope. A protective vest (made from the same material as bullet-proof vests) protects the rider's upper body from the bull's hooves and horns. Riders also wear spurred boots, chaps, and a cowboy hat. Some riders wear a helmet and/or a face mask.

Even with the precautions that riders take, injuries happen. It's not if a bull

AT A GLANCE

Salary Range

Winnings vary greatly. There are hundreds of rodeos around the country where the winner takes home $1,500 or more per event. Many of the top bull riders make more than $100,000 a year.

Education/Experience

None required, but attending a well-respected bull riding school might give you the advantage you need to be a top competitor.

Personal Attributes

Physically fit, good balance and coordination with quick reflexes, determination, strong mental attitude.

Requirements

Most of the top rodeo and bull riding organizations require you to become a member in order to compete in their events. You generally need to be 18 years old (or the age of majority in your state) and pay a membership fee. Different levels of membership have additional requirements.

Outlook

With the popularity of rodeos and bull riding on the rise, there may be opportunities for talented bull riders willing to work hard.

rider will be injured, it's when—and how badly. The most frequent injury is a concussion, but shoulder injuries are also very common. At some point during a career, almost every rider will suffer from some type of groin injury.

Before climbing onto a one-ton bull and competing against some of the best riders in the country, you'll want to get some training. Some riders start out participating in small, local competitions, learning from more experienced riders. Others attend a bull riding school. Depending on the school, students might have the opportunity to learn from a former champion bull rider. Many riders learn through a combination of bull riding school and competitions.

Top riders encourage people just starting out—whether they're men or women—to get the best training possible. This can spell the difference between a champion rider and someone who's just a competitor. Good training also teaches riders how to do things safely and correctly, which can mean the difference between life and death.

When your riding days are over, you might choose to stay active in bull riding by becoming a judge or an announcer. Some veterans become stock contractors—those who own bulls and rent them for bull riding events—or trainers, even opening bull riding schools of their own.

Pitfalls

One of the biggest pitfalls in bull riding is the injuries, which can be so bad that they can end your career—or worse. And until you start winning a number of competitions, it might be hard to support yourself with only your rodeo prizes.

Perks

You'll have the chance to travel to different rodeos and bull riding events, perhaps eventually competing throughout the United States. You'll also be participating in one of the most popular spectator sports in the country.

Get a Jump on the Job

Look for programs, schools, and other opportunities where you can learn the

Mike Moore, bull rider

Mike Moore's family never told him his dream was an impossible one, despite the fact that he grew up outside of Chicago. "My grandfather lived in the country and had some horses, and I always wanted to be a cowboy." Moore wasn't a likely riding prospect. He didn't grow up on the back of a bull the way many of his competitors did: He was a city kid who didn't start riding bulls until he was 17. Even though everyone except his family told him that a black guy from Illinois can't be a cowboy, Moore knew that was what he wanted to do.

Fortunately, he had a supportive family and a junior high dean of students with a side job as a stock contractor (someone who leases animals to the rodeo). "I pestered him as much as I could, just to be around him," Moore says. Eventually, the dean hired Moore at age 15 to work on his rodeo crew setting up for rodeo events and taking care of the livestock. By the next summer Moore was riding broncos and never looked back. A year later, at 17, Moore climbed onto a bull for the first time. "I'd never experienced anything like it," he says.

After high school, Moore went on to college to earn an associate's degree in animal science and a bachelor's degree in elementary education at a Wyoming college. Today, Moore is riding bulls for a living back home in Illinois, where he can be close to his family. Moore loves the people he meets and enjoys being his own boss. "I can set up my own schedule and do what rodeos I want to do," he says.

"Going to a good quality school is very important," advises Moore. "Learn how to do it right, from someone who knows … And when you're done [training], leave with a positive attitude and go at it wholeheartedly. Be prepared to be hurt, because no matter how good a rider you are, eventually it will happen."

basics of bull riding. There are several organizations for bull riders under 18 that, in addition to giving aspiring bull riders valuable experience, will offer young riders the chance to win cash prizes and scholarships.

DRAG RACER

OVERVIEW

You love cars, you love to tinker with them, and you love to drive them. Plus, you absolutely love speed. In fact, your motto is "the faster, the better." Chances are you might enjoy life as a drag racer.

Drag racing takes place on a quarter-mile strip—1,320 feet long, to be exact—and each race is between two cars that race side-by-side from a standing start. The losing driver in each race is eliminated; the winning driver goes on to meet the winner of another race, until there are only two drivers left. These two race for the championship of that particular event.

Each race is monitored for elapsed time and speed. Elapsed time (E.T.) clocks the start-to-finish time. Speed is measured in a 66-foot speed trap that ends at the finish line. The car with the lowest E.T. is the winner. As you can see, one of the keys to drag racing isn't just having a fast car but also being able to leave the starting line with the fastest reaction time. That can often mean the difference between victory and defeat. If your advantage off the starting line is significant enough, thanks to your quick reaction to the green light that starts the race, it's possible to win even if your opponent goes faster.

The highest level of drag racing—the races you see on television—is conducted by the National Hod Rod Association (NHRA) and the International Hot Rod Association (IHRA). The NHRA is the larger and more popular of the two series and conducts more than 20 national events throughout the country.

AT A GLANCE

Salary Range

Varies tremendously depending on experience and career wins. Top drivers can expect to earn about $300,000 a year, not including bonuses. Winning drivers at a national event of drag racing's top circuit, the National Hot Rod Association (NHRA), receive a first-place check. Drivers can also earn money based on their weekly standings in the season-long point races and from their sponsors, based on their finish in that particular week's race. Top earnings come at the end of the season, when the top 10 finishers in each of the NHRA's four divisions receive their share of the bonus pool. The winners' earnings go to their race teams, where the funds are divided on a percentage basis among the driver, pit crew members, and engine mechanics.

Education/Experience

You can learn the ropes by racing as an amateur at a local track, which typically offers a full slate of competition for a variety of car types. Also, there are several driving schools that give you a mix of classroom and on-track education. The Frank Hawley Driving School is the official school of the NHRA.

Personal Attributes

First and foremost, you need a sense of adventure, a passion for speed, and fearlessness. This is not a job for the faint of heart, because should you reach the top level—either the NHRA or the smaller International Hot Rod Association (IHRA)—you'll be traveling at speeds upwards of 320 miles per hour.

Requirements

You'll need a driver's license and an extensive knowledge of cars and how they work. The NHRA has a licensing program for every class, from entry level to the pros. Each driver is required to make a series of runs under close supervision for certification. As for the car that you'll race, it will have to be "street legal," which means it needs

(continues)

AT A GLANCE *(continued)*

seat belts, tires, and an exhaust system that conform to the rules of the class in which you're running. When you arrive at the track to race, it's likely that your car will be "teched" by an official to make sure it's eligible to race. Drivers are also required to wear a helmet to race.

Outlook

If you enjoy racing and get your thrills from flying down the track, you can have a great time racing at tracks in your area. But if your plan is to make it to the top, you can expect an extremely tight job market. The sport is very expensive, and you have to be the best of the best to attract a team willing to commit the financial resources it will take to get you behind the wheel and on the track.

Drivers in this series set out to win each individual event, and they try to earn as many points as possible to win the season-ending championship in their class.

There are four major professional classes in drag racing: Top Fuel, Funny Car, Pro Stock, and Pro Bike. Cars in each class have to comply with certain limits on weight, engine size, ground clearance, and wheelbase length. Top Fuel dragsters, the fastest of the four classes, have been clocked at more than 320 miles per hour. They reach that speed in less than five seconds, which is the time it takes to cover the quarter-mile track.

Racing at the NHRA level is a very expensive proposition because of the high cost of the equipment. But even if you never reach the top level of drag racing, the beauty of this sport is that you can race at an amateur level at a track in your area. The NHRA offers many dif-

ferent classes that allow amateur racers to compete. There are more than 35,000 licensed competitors who race at the amateur level at 140 tracks throughout the United States.

If you have a car that's considered "street legal" (able to pass inspection), and you're ready to go racing, the chances are good that there will be a classification for you. You're not going to get rich by racing on the weekends at your favorite track, but you will have an awful lot of fun.

Pitfalls

The danger posed by drag racing is a major risk for anyone involved in the sport. Even if you're an amateur who races on weekends, there's always that chance that you might crash. The higher up the ladder you go, the more likely it is that those crashes could be serious, because the speeds at which you'll race will increase. That said, the dragsters, like all cars used in auto racing, are built to be as safe as possible.

Perks

You'll be around cars that go fast, and you'll be able to work on their engines and do what you can to improve their performance. What could be better for a car/speed lover?

Get a Jump on the Job

The more experience you can get behind the wheel, the better. The NHRA sponsors a Junior Drag Racing League for kids from 8 to 17. The competition is usually divided by age group, and the cars are half-scale versions of Top Fuel dragsters with five-horsepower engines that travel as fast as 85 miles per hour. There are about 4,500 kids in the United States

Ashley Force, drag racer

Ashley Force has racing in her blood. Her father, John Force, is one of the best Funny Car drivers in NHRA history, with 13 NHRA Funny Car season championships. So it's no surprise that Ashley has become a drag racer herself.

"I grew up going to the drag races to watch my dad," Ashley says. "All our family vacations were at the drag races. So I got to know all the other teams and the other drivers. When I was old enough to drive a street car, for my 16th birthday, I went to Frank Hawley's Drag Racing school and got my race license (a present from my father) and it kinda went from there."

Ashley started racing in some of the entry-level, amateur divisions that compete at tracks throughout the country and steadily moved up. She raced the 2005 season in a Top Alcohol dragster on the racing series one level below the NHRA's top series, in which her father races. "Now I'm training to one day race against my dad in a Funny Car," says Ashley, who was a cheerleader in high school and went on to graduate from Cal State–Fullerton in 2003 with a degree in communications.

Ashley has done well enough in the Top Alcohol category to have several commercial endorsements. She was part of a national ad campaign for Oakley sunglasses, and Mattel, which sponsors her car, has an Ashley Force–like Barbie doll in stores throughout the country.

For Ashley, a typical day at the track starts early in the morning. She warms up the car and then meets with the fans. "In drag racing, fans are allowed in the pit area and we spend a lot of our time talking to them, signing autographs, and posing for pictures," she explains. "Also, there are responsibilities to our sponsors. We make appearances at their hospitality areas to sign autographs for their customers, which are some of the same things we do in the pit."

When it's time to race, she puts on a fireproof driving suit and helmet and the crew tows the car to the starting line. "I do the burnout," she says, "which is a procedure that heats up the tires so you get maximum traction, and then it's time to race. A good run in my class is 5.25 seconds [for the quarter mile] at 270 miles per hour."

"When we're not racing, we go home and do what anybody else would do," she says, "try to get caught up on laundry and house cleaning and on stuff at the shop, like answering e-mails from fans, writing thank-you letters, doing phone interviews with the media, and getting ready to go out again."

As you might expect, the best part of the job as far as Ashley is concerned is "going fast." She also loves being part of a team. Traveling, however, is a double-edged sword. She enjoys seeing different parts of the country, but on the other hand, it means she's away from her family and friends. "In this job, it's especially important to have a supportive family," Ashley says. "I see the people who don't stay in racing, whether they're crew members or drivers, and they're the ones who aren't there [at the track] with their families. All the drivers and team members that I see out here for the long run, their relatives are on the road with them, their families love drag racing, and they come to all the races that they can."

"I know, for me, my family is very important," she says. "Maybe some people could do it without their family, but I need to have them there with me. When my sisters Brittany and Courtney are there, and my mom, it just makes it a lot more fun."

(continues)

(continued)

If you're considering drag racing as a career, or even if you'd just like to make it a hobby, something to do on weekends with your friends, Ashley suggests that you take any kind of automotive courses you can. "When I was in school in California, my mom wanted me to take home economics, but I took auto and welding instead," she says. "I still can't cook, but I'm pretty good at going fast." She also recommends you attend college. "Even though I don't do a lot of things with my major [communications], a lot of people ask if I went through school and it seems to be important, especially to sponsors," she says. "So finish up school first. Then just go to the races and just meet people, talk to people on the teams."

Many drivers started out as crew members. "In fact, our other two drivers, Eric Medlen and Robert Hight, worked on my dad's Funny Car," she says. "Now they're driving the same kind of cars."

She also recommends that you consider going to a driving school. "That's what I did," she says. "I got licensed and then I started racing in one of the entry-level categories where you get really good experience. My dad says you have to know your race car inside and out. Mainly, you ask questions and you listen. That's what's worked for me."

involved in the program, and about 25 percent are girls. Each time you make a run, you're likely to learn something. So check out your local track, get your car ready to run, and then put the pedal to the metal.

GOLF BALL DIVER

OVERVIEW

There are 27 million adult golfers in the United States, according to the National Golf Foundation, an organization that compiles statistics and trends in the golf industry. Of those 27 million golfers, about 72 percent shoot scores of 90 or higher—and only about 8 percent shoot scores lower than 80. To put those numbers in perspective, Tiger Woods averages a score of less than 70.

This means there are a lot of golfers who don't hit the ball straight down the middle of the fairway. They hit it left, they hit it right, and sometimes they hit it into water. As if the game isn't difficult enough to master, golf course architects have made life even tougher for golfers by putting ponds, creeks, and streams in play.

If you hit a shot into the woods, there's a chance that with a keen eye and a little bit of luck, you can find it. But once your golf ball lands in the middle of a watery grave, it's most likely gone forever. But what's a lost golf ball to you is an opportunity for a golf ball diver.

Golf ball divers, who must be certified scuba divers, make a living by retrieving golfers' mistakes and then reselling them, either to golf courses or on eBay.

Typically, golf ball divers pay a golf course a small fee (between 5 and 10 cents) for each ball they find and for the right to go diving on that course.

Then, it's under the water to search for buried treasure. If you're in good shape and you're an excellent swimmer, you're off to a good start toward becoming a successful

AT A GLANCE

Salary Range

Salary depends upon the frequency of your dives, the number of balls you harvest, and the market in which you choose to sell the golf balls. eBay has proven to be one of the most effective places to sell golf balls. Golf courses also buy golf balls from divers. Prices for balls generally range from 50 cents to $3, depending upon the type of ball and its condition. The average daily haul for many divers is between 3,000 and 5,000 balls.

Education/Experience

A golf ball diver needs to be a well-conditioned athlete and an excellent swimmer. Strength is required to be able to dig balls out of the muck and then transport them from the water to the shore to your vehicle.

Personal Attributes

Being a golf ball diver is not for the faint of heart. In addition to being physically taxing, it also requires high pain tolerance, because cuts, bruises, and ear infections are part of the territory. And if you're claustrophobic, you might want to consider another way to make a living: Diving for golf balls is usually done in total darkness.

Requirements

First and foremost, you'll have to be certified as a diver by an organization such as the Professional Association of Diving Instructors. Kids from age 10 to 14 can get a junior certification; young adults older than 14 can be certified as an "Open Water" diver. You'll also need to be able to know your way around the Internet if you decide to sell your golf balls on eBay, and have a pleasant personality if you want to develop a relationship with golf pros at courses in your area.

Outlook

The outlook for golf ball divers appears to be good, as long as you're willing to work hard. It's estimated that golf ball diving is a $200 million industry in the United States.

Scott Lokken, golf ball diver

Scott Lokken makes his living by donning a wet suit, diving into the depths of dark, murky water, and searching for buried treasure. Sounds sort of glamorous and exciting, doesn't it?

Well, it's not quite what you think. Lokken doesn't explore sunken ships, looking for gold doubloons—he retrieves golf balls that don't reach their intended targets.

Lokken, who lives in Hudson, Wisconsin, dives for golf balls at 35 courses located throughout northern Minnesota and Wisconsin. For six months out of the year, he usually dives four or five days a week and averages about 5,000 balls a day. His one-day record is 21,000 balls, which took him 14 hours to gather, bag, and haul to his home. The balls weighed more than a ton.

After he collects the balls, he lugs them back home to his garage, where, with the help of his wife Kym and their three children, he washes and sorts them by brand and condition in order to sell, primarily on eBay or at his store, The Golf Ball Shop. He also sells some balls back to the courses at which they were found and sells others at flea markets. The average price for most balls he sells ranges from a dime to $1.50.

Lokken usually has between 10,000 and 20,000 balls on hand in his garage at any one time, although during the winter, his stash can grow to between 100,000 and 200,000 balls.

He's continuing a tradition that began with his father and uncle, who started diving for golf balls on a part-time basis in the 1930s in Minnesota. Lokken, now 44, first dove for golf balls in 1972 when he was 11 years old. The following year, he made $70 in one day, which he considered big bucks, compared to the $10 a week he made delivering newspapers. He was hooked. He became a full-time diver about 20 years ago.

His day begins at 5 a.m., and he's usually at a golf course by 6:30 a.m., diving between six and eight hours a day. He clears the waters at smaller courses once a year; at larger, busier courses, he shows up five or six times a year. Because of the frigid temperatures, he dives only half the year.

"The best part of the job is being able to work anywhere I want," Lokken says. "Since I work for so many golf clubs, I can choose where I want to be on any day. It's also an excellent workout and I feel great after a long dive day."

golf ball diver. But you also have to prepare yourself to work in virtually total darkness. Golf ball divers, who are able to see only several inches in front of their faces, recover their quarry by feel, rooting through the muck with their hands and depositing their finds in a mesh bag.

Not all golf ball divers wear gloves, because they tend to be clumsy and make searching more difficult. But going without gloves means you'll be more likely to suffer cuts and bruises to your hands. After all, there are more things than just golf balls residing in the water—you'll find things such as bottles with jagged edges and rusted golf club shafts that have been tossed in by frustrated golfers.

And let's not forget the marine life, which can range from fish and snapping turtles to snakes and alligators. Most times these animals aren't all that dangerous, but during mating season, they can become much more aggressive than usual. The presence of pesticides in many water hazards is also a danger to golf ball divers.

Diving for golf balls is not without the life-threatening danger facing all divers. Some have drowned when they've

Most of the balls Lokken recovers are Top Flites and Pinnacles, which are used by many average- to high-handicap golfers. But when he dives into the lakes at pricier golf courses or at country clubs, the balls he finds are generally more expensive, such as those made by Titleist and Callaway.

Besides golf balls, Lokken also has found three complete sets of clubs, expensive putters and drivers, a pair of golf shoes, beepers, hockey pucks, and a complete set of dishes that apparently had been tossed from the balcony of the clubhouse. He's also located a women's purse that turned out to be the final piece of evidence in a burglary. One of the sets of golf clubs he found contained the golfer's wallet inside the bag. When Lokken called him to return the clubs and wallet, he was told: "Mail me my wallet. You can keep the clubs."

In addition to treasure, there's treachery under the water as well. "Animals and fish will bump into you and it might scare you a little, but for the most part, they leave you alone," Lokken says. Occasionally, things don't work out quite so well. Lokken recalls a nasty run-in with a snapping turtle, which attached itself to his thumb as he emerged from the water. He had to endure a trip to the emergency room as a result of blood poisoning caused by a cut on his hand.

When Lokken dives, he uses a surface air compressor instead of a tank on his back. A tank is heavier and can restrict mobility and ability to rise to the surface quickly in case there's a problem. "[The surface compressor] is less bulky and if you do get into trouble, you can just drop your weight belt and you'll pop up to the surface like a bobber," he says.

But even though Lokken has taken every safety precaution he can, the need to be aware of the surroundings and the dangers involved remains his most important consideration. "You have to be careful every day," he says. "Every year or two, I hear about a golf ball diver drowning, usually by getting tangled in weeds. So if diving for golf balls sounds good—go for it. But be careful; I don't want to read about you."

gotten tangled in weeds, branches, or fishing line, and were unable to return to the surface. You must be on guard and aware of your surroundings every minute you're underwater.

Once the day's haul is complete (often averaging about 5,000 balls), you have to transport, wash, and sort the golf balls to prepare them for sale. Golf balls are categorized by their condition: AAA for balls in like-new condition; AA for balls with slight scuff marks, flaws, or personal markings; and shag grade for balls with more serious flaws. Fortunately, golf balls hold up underwater much better than baseballs or footballs would. Today's golf balls are painted with a base coat, much like what's used on cars, and then finished with a clear coat that water can't penetrate.

Pitfalls

This isn't a job for the faint of heart. A golf ball diver is subject to numerous cuts and bruises; encounters with snakes, turtles, fish, alligators, and other marine life; the presence of pesticides; and the prospect of putting in a day's work in conditions that approximate the dark of night. And because golf ball divers are independent contractors, be prepared to pay for your own health insurance and benefits.

Perks

If you're athletic, adventurous, and enjoy the outdoors and more specifically the water, then you might enjoy a career as a golf ball diver. You can enjoy the independence of being your own boss and setting your own schedule.

Get a Jump on the Job

The most important factors are getting into shape and improving yourself as a swimmer. Physical conditioning is paramount. You'll also need to learn how to scuba dive. Having some familiarity with golf courses in your area will also help. You'll have to forge relationships with golf professionals for the right to be able to dive at a particular golf course.

GOLF CADDIE

OVERVIEW

It used to be that being a caddie for a professional golfer was a gypsy-like existence for down-on-their-luck guys who partied hard, slept late, and showed up at the first tee a few minutes before their player was scheduled to tee off.

These days, however, being a caddie on a pro tour is looked at as a profession, not just a job. Caddies take pride in their occupation and consider themselves part of a team. Golfers regard them in that way, too. You'll often hear a golfer, when describing his or her round, say "we" decided to hit a 7-iron on that hole, or "we" thought the putt would break from right to left.

A caddie has many responsibilities and can be crucial to a player's success. One of the primary jobs is to be as familiar as possible with the golf course. The player will need to know the yardage to the hole, the placement of the flag on the green, the location of whatever trouble (bunkers, water, or trees) exists, and how the wind or other weather conditions might affect the shot. To pick up this knowledge a caddie will usually walk the course prior to the start of the tournament and make notes in the yardage book that's provided for each course. If a golfer has a question, the caddie better have the answer.

The caddie must be available for the golfer before and after the round for practice sessions on the driving range or the putting green. The caddie also makes sure the player's equipment is in good shape and that there are the correct number of

AT A GLANCE

Salary Range

Generally speaking, caddies, in addition to being paid a weekly wage, earn between 6.5 percent and 10 percent of what their golfer wins in prize money. Some golfers give their caddies 10 percent for a win, 8 percent for a top 10, and 6 percent for everything else.

Education/Experience

The more you know about golf, the better. Most caddies are good players themselves, and that experience goes a long way toward becoming an effective caddie.

Personal Attributes

You'll have to be a hard worker, very enthusiastic, and have a knack for knowing the right thing to say. Your player might look to you for encouragement or advice if things aren't going well. Another trait that will come in handy is attention to detail. Professional golf is a very exacting occupation, and it is up to the caddie to provide much of the information a player needs on the course.

Requirements

Sturdy shoulders and a strong back are the first things you'll need. There is no certification needed to become a professional caddie, but be sure to get as much experience as possible. One way to improve your resume is to join the Professional Caddies Association (PCA), which offers an apprentice program that covers all aspects of the job. The PCA also offers a Master Caddie program.

Outlook

Fair. Turnover can be high, and the job isn't all that glamorous. Unless you work for a successful pro, the pay doesn't figure to be all that great, either.

clubs in the bag. The Rules of Golf state that players are allowed to carry only 14 clubs. Carrying more than 14 results in a two-stroke penalty. A caddie who makes a mistake like that is likely to find himself out of work. Just ask Miles Byrne, who was caddying for Ian Woosnam in the 2001 British Open, one of golf's four major championships. Byrne failed to notice that Woosnam had an extra club in his bag. Woosnam was penalized two strokes and ended up losing the British Open by three.

During a round of golf, the caddie carries the bag; helps with club selection, if asked; cleans the clubs after each shot before replacing them in the bag; rakes the sand traps; and makes sure there is no undue movement by people in the gallery. He might be asked to help his player read putts and he also tends the pin, making sure to remove it from the cup prior to the ball getting there.

That's the physical part of being a caddie. Then there are the counseling duties that all caddies must perform. A caddie has to be a cheerleader of sorts—enthusiastic, encouraging, and upbeat. He has to know what to say and, more importantly, what not to say. If the player loses his temper or his focus, or gets down on himself for playing poorly, it's a caddie's job to get the player back in the game. That might be accomplished by a pat on the back or a kick in the pants. It's up to the caddie to know which will work best for his player.

Caddies are paid a percentage of what their player earns a week. Some also receive a base salary. The percentages vary among players, but most caddies earn between 7 percent and 10 percent of the golfer's take. So if you're lucky enough to work for a successful player, you could earn six figures a year.

On the other hand, if you work for a player who is struggling, you could struggle, too, when it comes time to pay the bills. Professional golf is one of the few sports in which players' earnings are based on their performance. Most pro tournaments have a cut, which reduces the competition to about 70 players for the final two rounds of the event. Players who don't survive the cut are not paid—and neither are their caddies.

Caddies also have to pay for their own health insurance, which can be a big chunk of their salaries, especially if they have families. There's no sick pay or caddie retirement fund, either.

Travel is part of the caddie's job. They usually have to drive from tournament to tournament and also have to pay for their meals and lodging.

Being a caddie can be a difficult job. There are tremendous responsibilities with no guarantees for the future. Golfers have changed caddies for no other reason than their need for a change. But if you love golf, enjoy the outdoors, and don't mind living on the edge, this might be just the job you're looking for.

Pitfalls

The biggest pitfall is the uncertainty of earnings and availability of work. The job involves considerable travel and working in sometimes inclement weather conditions while lugging a bag that can weigh as much as 40 pounds. You are also without job security.

Perks

You get the chance to work outside on golf courses that offer beautiful scenery. You will also be around golf all the

Colin Cann, caddie

When Colin Cann was 21 years old, a friend introduced him to a golfer who played on the Ladies European Tour (LET), the overseas counterpart to the Ladies Professional Golf Association (LPGA) here in the United States. Cann, who has a passion for golf, caddied for her in several LET events during his vacations from work.

"The following year, I wanted to see if I could make a go of being a caddie full time," Cann says. "So I left my job to work on the LET. Thankfully, everything went well, and here I am today."

Since those early days on the job as a caddie, when Cann wasn't sure how long he'd last or if he'd make the grade, he has come a long way. He is recognized as one of the most effective caddies on the LPGA Tour, and he has "looped,"—another term for caddying—for some of the best players in the game.

Cann worked with Annika Sorenstam for six years, who is regarded by many to be the greatest player in LPGA history. Sorenstam won 14 tournaments, including two U.S. Women's Opens, with Cann carrying her bag.

Despite their success, Sorenstam and Cann went their separate ways in 1999. It was a mutual decision and is not all that unusual among players and caddies. Sometimes a player feels the need to do something different just for the sake of it, or the caddie is looking for another opportunity.

After leaving Sorenstam, Cann went to work for Grace Park for one year, before he formed a successful partnership with Se Ri Pak that lasted four seasons. Pak became one of the top players in the world during her time with Cann, winning 18 LPGA Tour events, including two major championships. She even accumulated enough points to qualify for induction into the LPGA Hall of Fame.

At the start of 2005, Cann made another player switch, going from Pak to Paula Creamer, a rookie who had a terrific first year on tour in 2005 and is considered to be one of the next great players in the world.

Cann is the type of caddie who is very meticulous in his preparation, and who can give his player a lot of very precise and very exacting information. Some players don't want much input; others crave all the information they can get. Achieving a balance and knowing what help your golfer wants is part of the player-caddie relationship. The caddie has to know what to say, and in some cases, what not to say.

In addition to developing the chemistry that will allow the partnership to succeed, it's also important that caddies do their homework and be available for the player whenever needed.

"A typical day for me during a tournament would include arriving at the golf course at least an hour before I am to meet my player," Cann says. "That allows me time to check out the course conditions. Then I usually meet my player an hour and 15 minutes before the tee time so she can warm up. The round usually lasts four to five hours, and then we usually practice another 30 to 60 minutes before we go back to our hotels."

After a good night's sleep, the entire process repeats itself the next day. When the tournament is over, it's on to the next stop on the tour, usually by car in order to keep expenses down.

Cann says caddies negotiate an individual pay scale with their player. Most caddies are paid a base salary, ranging from $600 to $1,000 a week, to cover expenses, such as travel, food, and

(continues)

(continued)

lodging. On top of that base salary, they earn a percentage of their player's winnings—an average of about 7 percent.

As far as Cann is concerned, the best part of his job is the competition and being around the game that he loves. The worst part is being away from home, which is probably true for all caddies, who spend a lot of time on the road and living in hotel rooms.

But if that lifestyle appeals to you, and you love golf and have a sense of adventure, becoming a professional caddie is worth considering. Cann said there's "very little" you can do to prepare yourself in terms of any kind of formal education. "But with that said, you must have a good understanding of the game of golf," he says. "You need a strong attention to detail and a lot of patience."

He also suggests having a Plan B in place, just in case your career as a caddie doesn't pan out.

"This is not a profession with a lot of security, so get a good education in case it doesn't work out for you financially," he says. "To prepare yourself for success, you must have a good knowledge of the game, including the rules, strategy, shot-making, and swing techniques.

"To get an initial bag [job], get to know as many people in the industry as you can. If possible, try to pick up a bag on one of the mini tours or one of the qualifying school events [held for young players by the pro tours]."

time—a definite perk since most caddies love golf.

Get a Jump on the Job

Become a caddie at a local country club. Learn as much as you can about golf and golf courses, and pay special attention to the way experienced caddies at the club do their jobs—where they stand, what they do for their player after each shot, how carefully they rake sand traps, and their different tasks on the green.

GOLF COURSE ARCHITECT

OVERVIEW

If you play golf, chances are you've come upon a hole that has given you fits. No matter how many times you play it, and how hard you try, the result is the same: awful. Which leads you to mutter to yourself—or maybe even loud enough for others to hear—that if you were a golf course architect, you would've designed the hole completely differently. Maybe golf course architecture is in your future.

It's a job that requires an appreciation of golf; an eye for turning an undeveloped tract of land into 18 challenging, exciting, and visually appealing holes; and a varied education to help you deal with the many factors that you'll encounter.

Getting the proper education is extremely important. There are four educational components that are necessary: a background in design, studying landscape architecture, architecture, or engineering; experience in turfgrass management; a background in environmental science; and an apprenticeship to an experienced golf course architect.

As you can see, becoming a golf course architect doesn't happen overnight. It might take years to establish yourself, so patience is a virtue in this job.

Patience is also a virtue in the actual building of a golf course. You don't go from a wooded piece of property to an 18-hole golf course in a couple of weeks. The process, from start to finish, can take several years.

The process begins as the golf course architect walks the land, several times, to

AT A GLANCE

Salary Range

What you make depends on your experience, the number and quality of courses you've designed, and your fame. You can expect to start at about $20,000 a year as an associate with a golf course architecture firm. Should you develop into a lead designer with a fairly recognizable name, your salary could be in the $200,000-a-year range. The average salary for an architect with a few years experience is approximately $45,000.

Education/Experience

It's rare to find a college or university that offers a degree in golf course architecture, so a degree in landscape architecture is a popular choice among would-be golf course designers. Another route would be to major in civil or environmental engineering. You could also take classes in turfgrass management, horticulture, or agronomy.

Personal Attributes

A love of the outdoors, a willingness to work hard, and the ability to be inventive and imaginative when it comes to the land you'll be dealing with will all come in handy. It also helps to be likable, enthusiastic, and open-minded, because you'll have to sell yourself as well as your talent for golf course architecture to potential clients.

Requirements

As the job requires many different aspects, having a well-rounded education would serve you well. Interning or serving an apprenticeship under an experienced architect is also a way to gain experience. Once you've become an architect, joining a professional organization such as the American Society of Golf Course Architects will spruce up your resume and help you keep current on changing trends in the industry.

Outlook

Fair. According to research by Golf 20/20, a collaboration of organizations concerned with the future of the sport, there were fewer golf courses planned and opened in 2004 than at any time in the previous 16 years. This reflects a lack of demand in the marketplace, because participation has remained flat.

become familiar with its natural attributes. The best architects take advantage of the features that are already there—the hills, swales, ridges, forested areas, wetlands, and so on.

The architect sketches ideas for the course on a drawing pad or topographic map. After compiling notes into a rough draft, it's time to return to the office to begin routing the golf course, from the first hole to the 18th hole, plotting the location of tees, fairways, bunkers, and greens. Once that map is complete, it must be submitted to government agencies for their approval on matters dealing with the environment, soil conservation, and drainage. Before the bulldozers and backhoes begin, the routing plan is generated on a computer in order to make all the specifications concise and exact.

After all the preliminary work has been completed, it's finally time to start the job. Once the construction process begins, it's important for the architect to be available to answer questions and communicate his or her vision. The more hands-on the architect is, visiting the construction site, the more successful the project is likely to be.

No matter how precise the architect was with the routing plan, and no matter how carefully that plan was developed, problems or unforeseen circumstances are bound to arise. Maybe the addition of a bunker would add to the playability of the course, or maybe a tree creates too much shade to grow the grass properly on a green or a tee. Those are issues much easier to resolve if the architect is on the site as opposed to on a cell phone.

Golf course architects usually start their careers as apprentices. The role of an apprentice can be very important to the success of a project. Apprentices learn the business by observing the skills and qualities of a master architect. But more than just watching, they can also produce plans through the use of the computer and various software packages. And should more information be needed in a particular area—say, the specific details about the soil mixture needed for tees and greens— the apprentice might be assigned to gather all the information available and present it to the master architect, who would make the final decision.

And just in case you thought being a golf course architect meant not having to do paperwork—all the decisions and revisions made during the course of the project must be documented so that the client has a complete record of how the project unfolded.

There's also the not-so-small matter of the budget. Golf course construction is very expensive. The U.S. Golf Association estimates the cost of building an average golf course to range from $1.6 to $4.5 million, so it's important that the accounting procedures are followed carefully.

Pitfalls

Not every client is going to share your vision. You could spend days walking a piece of property, come up with what you believe is an exciting, innovative, and aesthetically beautiful design, only to have your client give you a thumbs down. It's best not to take those rejections personally; it's just a difference of opinion, and one of those things over which you have no control. That's not the only thing you don't control. Another downer in being a golf course architect are the weather-related delays in construction.

Perks

Imagine being able to transform a beautiful piece of land into an 18-hole golf

Kelly Blake Moran, golf course architect

Kelly Blake Moran started designing golf courses when he was 14 years old and growing up in Odessa, Texas. Moran was bitten by the golf bug early on. He began playing when he was 10 and started dabbling in design several years later, redesigning his home course—Odessa Country Club—for fun on notebook paper.

"From when I was about 14 years old through my senior year in high school, I would draw individual holes from my home course," he explained. "I'd add features like bunkers and ponds. So clearly, at an early age, I knew that the design world existed."

After graduating from high school, he attended Texas A&M University, majoring in landscape architecture, because he thought it gave him the best background for becoming a golf course architect.

While at A&M, two professors—both of whom had been involved in golf course architecture—supported his decision to enter the field. When he visited a golf course under construction with one of his classes, he was so intrigued by the design that he contacted the architect—von Hagge Design Associates—to learn more about the project. Moran must have made quite the impression, because 10 days after he graduated from A&M in 1984 with a bachelor's degree in landscape architecture, he was hired by von Hagge Design Associates as an apprentice, eventually becoming a full partner.

Moran could have remained with von Hagge, probably moving up the corporate ladder to the administrative level, from where he would assign projects and jobs to second- and third-level employees. But that wasn't what he was looking for. He didn't want to delegate; he wanted to design. So in 1995, Moran went out on his own and opened his own design firm, which bears his name.

"I guess I feel there is something about the integrity of this business—that if you are the person putting your name out there, you should be the person who is doing the work," Moran says. There's no question that Moran does the work when he takes on the job of designing a golf course. He is a proponent of what's called land-based design, a concept that puts him at the center of everything—design and implementation.

Not everyone, of course, sees golf course design the way Moran does, which leads to some frustration. "Probably the moments that most disturb me are when you can not convince someone

(continues)

course that you conceived, designed, and turned into a reality. If you love golf and are a creative and imaginative person who doesn't mind hard work and long hours, being a golf course architect could be the ultimate occupation.

Get a Jump on the Job

Visit as many golf courses as you can, especially those considered among the best in the country, to develop an appreciation for golf courses and what went into their design and construction. Talk to golf professionals and golf course superintendents about their courses and how and why they turned out the way they did. It also wouldn't hurt to get a job as a member of the grounds crew to learn about the maintenance involved.

that you are the right person for their project," he says. "That moment when you realize that the person with whom you are communicating is not swayed by your presentation of the special ways you approach design. That's discouraging, especially when you get the feeling that they think all golf course architects are the same. As an architect who is constantly striving to do better, to seek new ways to present strategic challenges, you really do not view yourself as just the same as everyone else."

But if the client does hire Moran, it's a given that he'll be a hands-on designer from the start. Moran makes numerous site visits to the property he's going to develop. He walks the land, becomes familiar with its features and visualizes how the golf course will unfold, paying special attention to how he can best take advantage of the land's natural surroundings. Usually, Moran settles on the location of the 18 greens and then works backwards to the tees, all the while trying to give the golfer a design that is exciting, innovative, and enjoyable.

"The most enjoyable part of my profession is the creative adventures in the field when a course is under construction," he says. "The interaction with the shapers in the field, the quiet moments contemplating the design while standing on a proposed green or tee location, all are special moments because of the exciting potential that you know will eventually become a golf hole."

Moran has designed golf courses in Pennsylvania, New Jersey, New York, Florida, Chile, Argentina, Uruguay, and Mexico. He also did renovation work at Isleworth Country Club in Windermere, Florida, which happens to be the home course of none other than Tiger Woods.

For students who would like to make golf course design their career, Moran offers this advice: Develop an appreciation for the natural characteristics of the land. Hike, camp, and spend time looking at natural land and noting what you find intriguing and stirring.

Make notes on your thoughts after playing better courses, and be especially sensitive to what made the holes exciting to play.

Listen to what people say about courses, and don't be quick to judge the merits of the course or the accepted opinions about the course.

"And always seek to be fully creative in everything you do," Moran says. "In other words, don't become routine in your approaches. Seek creative solutions to every little and big thing you do in the profession. Clients want your unique, creative approach, not a copy of someone else's approach. Allow yourself to grow and accept some ideas or theories that you originally rejected. Listen to what others say about the various aspects of a golf hole or golf course that especially excite them, and try to learn more about their thoughts.

"All of this research, listening, and contemplation will mix together and form a solid basis for your own creative approach to golf course design. But remember that it is a process. You don't reach the point of knowing everything there is to know after just a couple of years in the profession. Hopefully it is an ongoing process throughout your career."

GOLF PRO

OVERVIEW

When most people hear that somebody has a job as golf professional, they think that person spends most of his or her day at the driving range or the practice putting green, giving lessons. And to be sure, one of the primary duties of a golf professional is teaching the game to people of all ages. But that's just one of many things on the job description.

A golf pro has to organize tournaments and outings; run the pro shop, including ordering and displaying the merchandise; set up instructional programs for individuals, groups, men, women, and juniors; manage the fleet of golf carts; know the Rules of Golf; and be of service to members and customers at all times.

The one thing golf pros don't get to do a whole lot of is play golf themselves, because they're usually too busy taking care of everyone else's golf games.

Becoming a golf pro involves going through an intensive program that involves everything from business courses to teaching techniques to an on-course playing ability test. While the Ladies Professional Golf Association offers certification through its LPGA National Teaching Division, the most popular—and respected—certification program is the one run by the Professional Golfers Association of America (PGA).

The PGA's Professional Golf Management Program (PGM) is open to college graduates who have earned a four-year degree and to college students attending one of the 17 schools that offer the courses as part of their curriculum.

Mark Anderson, golf pro

If Mark Anderson had had his way, he would be playing baseball for the Boston Red Sox these days, instead of making his living as PGA Class A head golf professional at Heidelberg Country Club in Bernville, Pennsylvania.

When he was 14 years old, growing up in Braintree, Massachusetts, all he wanted to do was play baseball. That was his dream. Golf wasn't even on his radar and he didn't know the first thing about the game. But then his brother and a friend decided they were going to attend a free junior golf clinic at a public course about a mile from Anderson's house. "To be honest, I didn't even know the course was there," Anderson recalls. "The only reason I went to the clinic was because I was so competitive. I figured if my brother and his friend were going to try something, well I figured, 'If you can do it, I can do it, too.' "

To this day, Anderson can remember that day, which took place more than 20 years ago. The group was split into two, and he was given a five-iron and told to hit a shot.

"The shot was from about 130 yards and I put the ball right on the green," he says. "The pro who ran the clinic gave me a golf ball for hitting such a good shot, which I thought was the coolest thing."

From there, Anderson was hooked on golf. He never planned on going out for the golf team as a sophomore, but when he heard that other team members were shooting the same scores he was, he decided to give it a shot. He made the team, getting the last spot on the roster.

The following year, Anderson played No. 2 on the team, and during his senior year, he moved up to No. 1.

His college choice was Florida Southern in Lakeland, Florida, a Division II school that had one of the premier golf programs in the country and had won the national championship the previous year. Anderson was allowed to practice with the team, but wasn't good enough to crack the lineup, which included Lee Janzen, who has gone on to win two United States Open Championships.

Deciding he'd rather play than just practice, Anderson transferred to Indiana University of Pennsylvania, also a Division II school. He had a solid career at IUP and even won the long drive contest at the NCAA Division II national championships. He also graduated with a degree in business management, which would come in handy when it came to making it through the requirements for becoming a PGA Class A golf professional.

Anderson had to graduate from two PGA business schools and pass a Playing Ability Test. He earned his Class A status in August 1996. The road to becoming a PGA pro these days is different. It's tougher and "more intense," says Anerson, who also believes that it's a better program because it weeds out candidates who aren't quite up to the challenge.

Before you can apply to the PGM program, however, you must demonstrate that you know how to play the game. The Playing Ability Test (PAT) is one of the first and most important steps in becoming a PGA golf professional. The test has to be completed within two years prior to registering for a PGM program.

The PAT consists of 36 holes (two rounds) and passing it means scoring equal to or less than the target score. In case you're interested, the target score is determined by multiplying the U.S. Golf

And being a head pro is a challenge. There are a variety of responsibilities that require organizational skills, business and merchandizing acumen, and the ability to keep your members and/or customers happy.

"You have to know a lot about business and have a pretty good business sense," Anderson says. "You're running a retail operation, if you have anything to do with the pro shop, and most pros do. So you have to be very good at merchandising; you have to meet with sales reps to pick out what clothing to stock and what hard goods [clubs, balls, etc.] to bring in. You also have to be able to formulate a business plan and handle a budget."

It can be a lot of work. Anderson, who is married and has a 2-year-old son, admits the six-day weeks and the 10- to 12-hour days during the golf season can be draining. But not enough to have lessened his love for the job.

"I'm in a situation where people are happy to be here [at the club]," he says. "They're leaving whatever problems they have. They want to forget them, come to the golf course, and have a good time. Everyone around here is here to have a good time. I can't imagine a better working environment than that."

In a perfect world, Anderson would have more time to play golf. Because of his duties at the club, however, the most he can expect to play is two or three times a week.

If you decide that you'd like to pursue a career as a head golf professional, Anderson offers this advice: "You have to love the game of golf and you have to really enjoy being around people. If you're not a people person, you're really going to struggle being a golf pro, especially at a private course where you tend to see the same people each day. The other thing is to figure out what you want to do: Do you want to work at a private club, a public course, be a teaching pro? Then find an established facility that coincides with what you want to do.

"If you want to be the head pro at a private club, then you want to go to the best private club you can find and get a job there. Even if you have to be the third assistant [pro] or work the driving range for a year. If you want to be a teaching pro, then go work for a famous teacher, even if you have to pick up range balls. It will be much easier to get a good job if you have big names on your resume.

"You could be the greatest guy in the world, but if your resume says you've come from a public course, the members [at the club you're applying to] are going to say, 'Why did you hire him?'

"That really does make a big difference. You might struggle in the short term, but you'll be much better off in the long term."

Association course rating by two and then adding 15 strokes.

So let's say you planned to take your PAT at Pebble Beach Golf Links in Pebble Beach, Calif. Pebble Beach has a course rating 72.3, which, multiplied by two equals 144.6, and adding 15 strokes puts the target score at approximately 160. That means your 36-hole score would have to be 160 or less, which means shooting a pair of 80s. According to the PGA, fewer than 20 percent of those taking the PAT pass it. So make sure to practice hard before teeing off.

Once you pass your PAT, you're ready to tackle the PGM courses. The PGM is a four-and-a-half-year program that provides extensive classroom studies and an internship experience, which lasts at least 16 months at a golf industry location. Students choosing the PGM program as a major can earn degrees in anything from marketing or business administration to recreation or park management.

If you're going to choose the college route, here are two things you should know. First, getting into the program depends upon satisfying the entrance requirements of the particular college you choose. Second, each college allows there to be a total of only 300 people in the program at one time and admits only 100 students each year.

The PGM consists of three levels, each focusing on different aspects of the golf industry. It is a self-paced program, which means if you are diligent and can manage your time wisely, the PGA reports that some people have completed the entire program in as little as 13 months. A more realistic expectation is 16 to 18 months to complete Level 1, about 12 months to complete Level 2, and another six months to a year to complete Level 3. That makes the overall time frame about three years.

Once you successfully complete the PGM program, you can expect it to take an additional five years to move up the ladder to become the head professional at a golf course or facility. And not everyone completes the PGM program. The PGA says that approximately 40 percent of apprentices leave the program within the first two years.

Pitfalls

During the golf season, you can expect to work six days a week, including weekends and holidays, and from 50 to 70 hours a week. Being a golf professional starts at dawn and doesn't end until dusk. If you're married, it would be a huge bonus to have an understanding spouse. You also might have to consider getting another job or moving south for the winter, if you happen to work at a club that closes until spring.

Perks

You get to be around golf and people who love to play it. You will also have motivated students who will look to you as the savior of their golf swings.

Get a Jump on the Job

The first thing to do is become proficient at playing the game and then become a student of the game so you can teach others. It wouldn't be a bad idea to take lessons from a number of different professionals to learn about their teaching styles and techniques.

GOLF TOURNAMENT DIRECTOR

OVERVIEW

Golf tournaments on any of the major professional tours in the United States last for three or four days, generally starting on a Thursday or Friday and ending on a Sunday. Prior to the start of the tournament, a pro-am event, which features a pro golfer paired with four amateurs, takes place for one or two days.

Okay, so you're thinking: "Wow, that's a pretty cool job. You get to spend a week running a professional golf tournament, you get to meet the players, you do some interviews with the media, and hand out the trophy and the first-place check at the awards ceremony after it's all over. Plus you get paid for it. How tough could one week be?"

In reality, tournament week is probably the easiest part of the job. That's because, if you're an effective tournament director, you've spent most of the last year getting everything ready so that the event runs smoothly.

Professional golf tournaments require the better part of one year to prepare for. It takes a tournament director who is on top of things—many, many things—and a staff that also knows what they're doing. So perhaps the first task of a tournament director is to hire talented assistants who can be trusted to work hard.

Hard work and organization are key to running a successful event. You need to be extremely organized and pay attention to every detail. Of the hundreds of details

AT A GLANCE

Salary Range

If you work as the tournament director of a golf event on one of the pro tours, you can expect to earn anywhere from $80,000 to $120,000 a year.

Experience/Education

Although there's no law demanding it, having an undergraduate degree in business management, sports management, or marketing would be a huge help. You'll also need some experience in public relations and extensive knowledge about golf and golfers.

Personal Attributes

Much of your job is going to entail dealing with the public, so a pleasant, upbeat, and enthusiastic personality is a must. You're not going to persuade too many people to get involved with your event if you're Oscar the Grouch. You'll also need to be hardworking and very organized.

Requirements

There are no classes or certifications needed to be tournament director of a professional golf event.

Outlook

There are four major golf tours in the United States—the PGA Tour (men), the LPGA Tour (women), the Champions Tour (senior men), and the Nationwide Tour (developmental tour for men). Each of those tours has a finite number of tournaments, so the job market for tournament directors is tight. There are various mini tours throughout the United States that need tournament directors, but such work is generally part time.

that have to be dealt with over the course of your preparation, one of the most important is knocking on doors and asking business owners and community leaders for money. It takes a great deal of money to prepare a successful golf tournament. Each tournament is usually sponsored by a

JoAnn Heller, golf tournament director

For nine years, the CoreStates/First Union/Wachovia Betsy King Classic (the name changes were due to bank mergers) had a spot on the LPGA schedule, and for the last eight of those years, JoAnn Heller served as the tournament director.

Heller, who is an accomplished golfer, has been around the game for her entire life, and when it came time to appoint a new tournament director after the event's first year, she was an obvious choice.

"The first year of the tournament, I was an assistant to the tournament director, so I learned the ins and outs of the tournament scene," Heller says. "Plus, my degree in business management was a big help."

Heller guided the tournament, held at Berkleigh Country Club in Kutztown, Pennsylvania, through the aforementioned name changes, date changes, and weather extremes—from the stifling humidity of late August to the frost delays in mid-October. But the tournament ran smoothly each year because Heller was in control of all those things she was able to control.

The key to Heller's effectiveness as a tournament director was her meticulous preparation, which was an ongoing process throughout the year.

"In the offseason, the first nine months I would solicit businesses for sponsorship," she explains. "The average LPGA event needs between $4 and $5 million to make money for charity.

"Six months out, I secured all the contracts for the operations side of the event—Port-a-Potties, trailers, tents, catering, etc. Three months out, my volunteer coordinator gathered 1,000 volunteers and the person in charge of the pro-ams got set for our three pro-am events. One month out I solidified everything with the television network [The Golf Channel]."

But the real fun took place the week before the event, which Heller called "advance week." Here's a day-by-day rundown of her responsibilities: On Monday, LPGA officials arrive on site to set up the golf course; tents and bleachers begin to go up; trailers are delivered and put in place; all two-way radios are assigned. On Tuesday, pro-am gift packs for the amateur participants are assembled; the floors are assembled for all the tents that will be used; and all the fencing is put

major company, which has its name in the event's title, such as the Buick Invitational, the Mercedes Championship, or the John Deere Classic. These sponsors guarantee most of or all of the total prize money available to players.

But there are lots of expenses associated with running a golf tournament; expenses for tents and bleachers and the rental fee for the golf course, to name a few. The tournament director has to solicit funds from other businesses to offset those costs. Money also comes in from amateurs wanting to play in the pro-am. The whole idea of the golf

tournament is to turn a profit—hopefully a big profit—because all the proceeds of a pro golf tournament are donated to the charity or charities selected as beneficiaries.

For example, since 1938, the PGA Tour has raised nearly $1 billion for charity. It was expected to exceed $1 billion sometime in 2006.

As you can see, fund-raising is a critical part of a tournament director's job. It's such a major part of the job that if you're not comfortable asking people for money, you might think twice about whether this is the job for you.

up. On Wednesday, Port-a-Potties are delivered and put in place; corporate and merchandise tents are set up; and The Golf Channel arrives and begins laying cable. On Thursday, corporate and merchandise tents are carpeted; the admissions area is set up; and the operations company arrives to rope and stake the gallery and parking areas. On Friday, all concession trucks are put in place; the merchandise tent is stocked; and the parking lots are roped off. On Saturday, tent and bleacher set-ups are finalized; the media center is organized; and the merchandise tent is completely stocked. On Sunday, cash registers and credit card machines are installed; final details for the Monday pro-am are settled; and the admissions areas are completed.

The week of the tournament brings a whole different set of concerns, most of which are individual situations that have to be dealt with as they arise.

"You can expect 10- to 12-hour workdays three months out, and 18- to 20-hour workdays during advance week and tournament week," Heller says. "There is a lot of satisfaction when everything comes together, but there are also a lot of headaches leading up to tournament week."

Heller says that young people wanting to become tournament directors should have a degree in sports management and a lot of experience in the golf industry.

"You also need to have a good personality and be able to multitask," she says. "At any given time, I would have seven or eight people coming at me, so you have to be able to prioritize the importance of each question and act accordingly. Also, hire good people, because they make your job so much easier."

The least appealing aspect of the job, according to Heller, was having to go meet with business leaders with her hand out. "I really disliked raising money," she says.

But overall, she found the experience rewarding. "I liked the operations end of the tournament, getting everything set up and seeing the whole thing come together," Heller says. "And I liked the pressure of running the event. When it was all said and done, it was great to have pulled it off."

Most of the fund-raising takes place months before the tournament begins. As the months and weeks dwindle, more and more of the tournament director's energy is spent on logistical matters—everything from signage to the tournament program, from tickets to parking.

Another important consideration is securing the best golfers you can to play in your event. The better the quality of the field participants, the more likely lots of fans will show up to see the tournament. And more fans mean more tickets, concessions, and merchandise are sold, which is great for the bottom line. It's not unusual for a tournament director to travel to other tour events in order to convince players to play in his or her event. Building relationships with players, especially the most popular players, can go a long way toward making sure you have the best participants possible.

In addition to soliciting sponsors and attracting the best players, the tournament director also has to make sure the media get what they want in order to cover the event properly. Newspaper, television, and radio coverage lets people know what's going on with your event, when it's going on, and who it's going to be going on with. The better the media coverage, the more likely it is that fans will want to attend.

During the week of the event, the tournament director arrives at the course early and is usually one of the last to leave. It's his or her responsibility to make sure the players, fans, and sponsors are satisfied and happy. If they're not, then it's the job of the tournament director to resolve any issues that arise and make sure that everything runs smoothly. The tournament director, who is on call from arrival to departure, is never separated from a walkie-talkie that keeps the lines of communication open constantly. He or she is almost always outside, flitting from one place to another in a golf cart, trying to fix this or solve that.

After the event ends, the tournament director has to supervise the tear-down and cleanup of the host course. All money has to be accounted for and distributed to the beneficiaries; bills have to be paid; thank-you notes have to be written; and an assessment of what went well and what didn't has to take place.

And then, before you know it, the whole process starts over again, in order to get ready for next year's tournament.

Pitfalls

The job entails long hours, intense periods of what seems like nonstop work, and a variety of responsibilities. There is a lot at stake, because you have to please the players, make the event fun for the fans, and deliver what you hope is a big check to the charities. If you don't stand up well to pressure, this might not be the job for you.

Perks

You wouldn't choose to run a golf tournament unless you had a passion for the game, so being able to be around the game as a tournament director is a real plus. The chance to do something that benefits your community and charitable causes also makes for a great sense of fulfillment and satisfaction in one's work.

Get a Jump on the Job

Try to learn as much as you can about golf and the business of running a tournament. Every pro golf tournament needs volunteers to perform any number of tasks, whether it's carrying a scoreboard, directing traffic, being a gallery marshall, or answering phones. Filling one of these volunteer positions will give you an insiders' view into running a tournament.

GRAND PRIX DRESSAGE RIDER

OVERVIEW

The sport of Grand Prix dressage is a sort of elegant, slow-motion dance featuring a complete union between rider and horse. The precise movements of dressage require enormous strength and training on the part of the horse, and Grand Prix is the highest level of dressage to which a rider can aspire. In order to compete in a Grand Prix class, a horse must be able to complete a number of dressage tests. These include the *piaffe*, a calm, composed trot executed all in one place, and *passage*, a movement done while trotting with an elevated stride, seeming to pause between steps. Gaits include the *collected gaits*, a shortened stride at the trot and canter, with the hindquarters collected underneath and more weight on the back end, and the *extended gaits*, a lengthened stride at the trot and canter, with great forward thrust and reach. A horse also needs to be able to make *flying changes* (one and two tempis), in which the horse changes leads at every stride (one tempi), two strides (two tempi), or three strides (three tempi) while cantering. The horse also needs to be able to perform a *pirouette* at the canter and a *half-pass*, a sideways, forward movement while bent slightly in the direction of movement.

A rider reaches Grand Prix competition by slowly moving the horse up the levels at different shows until the horse has learned all the movements listed previously, which are required at the Grand Prix level. Tech-

AT A GLANCE

Salary Range

Varies considerably but is typically very low; prize money may cover costs of entry fees, which can be more than $1,000. Dressage riders earn a living by teaching others the sport, training Grand Prix horses, and buying and selling Grand Prix horses.

Education/Experience

While there is no educational requirement, years of training are required to be able to ride at this level of competition. Most Grand Prix dressage champions begin riding at age five or six, but only begin to learn dressage in late adolescence or early adulthood. Learning the complicated dressage moves continues throughout the rider's life.

Personal Attributes

Love and understanding of horses, patience, attention to detail, meticulousness, willingness to work hard.

Requirements

Excellent horseback riding experience in the precise movements of dressage.

Outlook

Fair. This sport has gathered momentum over the past decade and become more popular, but the number of individuals with the ability, training, talent, funds, and opportunity to compete is limited.

nically, there aren't any restrictions in an open show, so anyone could ride a horse in a Grand Prix level class, but if the horse can't do the moves the score won't be good. Horses usually hit their peak at age 11 or 12, and they can remain competitive until about 16 or 17; after that, their abilities begin to decline.

Grand Prix dressage riders usually start riding as a child. You've first got to master riding and start attending shows, where you learn how to control the horse

Barbie Ulbrich, Grand Prix dressage rider

Just like lots of girls across the country, Barbie Ulbrich started riding as a child—she was just 3 years old when she started riding on the farm where she grew up. "I always rode," she says, "from the time I can first remember." So it was no surprise that little Barbie would want to aim for an equine-related career.

She started college at Lake Erie College in Painesville, Ohio, riding and jumping, but midway through she was introduced to dressage, and switched her focus. "They had a school horse there that could do the flying changes every few strides—they look like they're skipping. I thought: 'Yes! This is for me!' It was such a great feeling. Also, I was riding jumpers at the time, and when the jumps got to six feet I didn't have the nerve to continue. So I was more open to a new venue. Plus riding dressage involves a lot of meticulous work, which suits my personality."

She graduated with a B.S. in equestrian studies, and her parents presented her with a half-trained dressage horse to train. "In our sport, so much depends on your horse—you're only as good as your current horse." It's what makes the sport so expensive: a fully trained Grand Prix horse—if you can find one for sale—can cost $500,000. Even a partially trained animal might fetch $50,000. And unlike Grand Prix jumpers, who often ride horses belonging to others, most Grand Prix dressage riders own and ride their horses.

After graduation, Ulbrich moved to Austria to train, where she lived in Vienna for three years, studying with a horseman from the Spanish Riding School. Her goal was to perfect her riding. "I think in back of their minds, every rider wants to be on the Olympic Team. It's stronger for some of us than others. In my mind, my goal has always been to be as good a rider as I can. That meant moving up the levels to Grand Prix, but it's always a gamble. It's not just if the rider is going to be good enough—it's whether the horse is good enough. You never know. I've had two horses since that Grand Prix horse who haven't made it. It's not for lack of skill of the trainer, it's just that they weren't suited to it." It may take four years of training before the rider discovers her potential Grand Prix horse isn't quite going to cut the mustard—and so it's back to the beginning with another horse and start all over again.

Ulbrich made the U.S. equestrian team in 1997 on a horse she trained herself, but she hasn't yet been in the Olympics. "Sometimes I think people who make the team are those who do the paperwork right," she laughs. "There are very complex rules." There are different competitions every year, and there are the Olympics every four years. Every year there is the World Cup; for each of those, the U.S. fields an equestrian team. There are different criteria at different shows and a minimum score you have to achieve, followed by one final tryout competition where they choose the best 10, by a pick of the top four in the country. "You definitely have to march right along to get good enough scores to be there, so they are sure they can send the strongest team they can send," Ulbrich says.

It's a long process, but fortunately it's a forgiving sport. Unlike gymnastics, where most athletes are washed up by their late teens, Grand Prix dressage riders can still compete into their 60s. "As

and work together as a team. As you get older, if you're talented enough and you find a well-trained horse, you may begin the arduous trek toward progressing through various dressage levels to reach the Grand Prix class. This level brings the

you get older, your physical ability begins to decline," she says, "but this sport takes so long to learn that your knowledge is valuable. Maybe you can't ride as strongly as you did when you were younger, but you ride smarter. You have the luxury of spending a long time continuing to compete."

If you're dreaming of a Grand Prix career, Ulbrich suggests you get a job working for someone already in dressage at that level, so you know what it takes to get there. "It's important to take that person's advice," she says. "I see an awful lot of people trying to make it with an unsuitable horse. People can waste five or 10 years on a horse that won't be able to move up the levels so you can't learn the upper level stuff."

You also must be realistic about the kind of salary you'll earn—which is not much, at least from Grand Prix competition itself. Ulbrich teaches adult dressage students at her Starbound Farm in Maryland. Because of its meticulous nature, dressage is not a sport that kids typically enjoy, she says. "As a kid, you want to have a good time, jump over fences. The difference between jumping and dressage is like the difference between jump rope and chess. As a kid, you don't want to sit there and figure out chess moves."

The money she earns at her farm comes from training other horses, teaching riders, and buying and selling trained animals. "In my most successful year, my horse paid his entry fees by winning prize money." You might spend $1,000 in entry fees at just one big show. "It's nice to win that back so you don't have those expenses," she says. "At the biggest shows they offer prize money, but the smaller shows don't offer money at all."

Typically, Ulbrich will go to Florida in the winter to compete at a number of shows there, and then back to the East Coast to compete at shows closer to home, hitting the biggest shows in the fall.

At the moment, she doesn't have a Grand Prix horse. "I'm beginning to think that the 8-year-old I own isn't going to make it. At some point, I'll have to re-evaluate." This is one of the toughest, most painful parts of the sport, she says. "You've put four years into them and you love them, and it's usually a very emotional decision. That's what trips up a lot of people. Even though they know the horse won't make it, they keep the horse because they love him. If you want really super horses, you have to get rid of those who aren't super, even if you love them."

There's really nothing about the sport that Ulbrich doesn't like, "but the struggle to get there and maintain it is difficult. You train a horse, they're great, and then they retire, and you have to start all over. With each horse you learn more, but you have to love the process, because you can't live for the result or you'll be disappointed most of the time."

Despite the drawbacks, Ulbrich loves the feeling she gets when everything is in harmony with her horse. "When it really works, it's such a fantastic feeling," she says. "It's a fleeting feeling, but that's what keeps me going. It doesn't even have to be on a Grand Prix horse, but all of a sudden they understand what you want and the two of you become one. It's not the blue ribbon, it's that elusive feeling."

most difficult, challenging moves required by horse and rider that can take years to master.

As a dressage rider, you must love working on making a circle perfect. So much of a rider's work is in muscle building, and working on transitions between gaits. Grand Prix dressage riders must be meticulous, very patient, and spend a lot of time doing very simple exercises and trying to perfect them. Your days will be filled with practice and training as you prepare for various Grand Prix shows across the country.

If you dream of becoming a Grand Prix dressage rider, you can either buy your own fully-trained Grand Prix–caliber horse (costing at least $500,000) or you can go with a much younger, green horse (around $50,000) and train him yourself. Of course, there's a risk—you won't really be able to tell if he's Grand Prix material until he's about 10 years old, after you've already invested lots of time and money over the years on his training.

Ultimately, success on the Grand Prix dressage circuit may lead to a spot competing for the U.S. Equestrian Team or (every four years) on the U.S. Olympic team—*if* your horse is good enough.

The sport of Grand Prix dressage is much bigger in Europe than in the United States, with Germany, the Netherlands, and Denmark the leading countries in the sport, although Spain and the United States are also quite competitive.

Pitfalls

There's very little money in this field—and even if you're an Olympic rider, you won't get the sort of fame and lucrative endorsements that you would if you were a successful gymnast, for example. It can be enormously frustrating and even painful to buy and train a horse for years, becoming personally attached, only to realize that he'll never really be good enough to compete on the Grand Prix circuit. Your only choice at that point is to sell him and start all over again at the very beginning. Even if you manage to train a real winner, who captures Grand Prix gold, he'll only be able to maintain that level for about four or five years. After that, you'll need to retire the horse and start all over again.

Perks

For the athlete who loves horses and dressage, there can be no more exciting career than competing on the Grand Prix circuit. Mastering the complex movements of dressage can take years, so finally reaching that level is enormously satisfying.

Get a Jump on the Job

It's never too early to start riding, so if you're interested in this field, get started as soon as you can. Hang around the barn, soak up all the horsemanship you can, and take as many lessons as you can afford. You may be able to exchange barn work at a local stable for lessons or riding time. If you can buy your own horse, great; otherwise, look into leasing a horse for practice. Many experts recommend studying dressage in Europe, where Grand Prix dressage riders are much more venerated and earn much more money.

HOCKEY PLAYER

OVERVIEW

Numbers may not lie, as the old saying goes, but they don't always make perfect sense, either. Despite the decline of the game from a fan's standpoint—due in part to a labor dispute that canceled the entire 2004–05 season—the number of boys and girls playing hockey in the United States has been on the rise. According to statistics compiled by the National Federation of State High School Federations, schools sponsoring boys' ice hockey teams have increased by 11.4 percent between 2001 and 2004. The number of boys participating in ice hockey has risen 9.3 percent over the same time period.

Girls' ice hockey isn't a sponsored high school sport yet, but in 2000 the National Collegiate Athletic Association made women's ice hockey an official sport. Like the men, the women also have a season-ending national championship tournament, culminating with the Frozen Four.

The path to becoming a professional hockey player can be long, difficult, expensive, and wearing. It takes a major commitment of time and money from the family, as well as a lot of determination and focus from the child who's playing.

The equipment alone costs a small fortune. You'll need a helmet; skates; elbow, shin, and shoulder pads; pants, shirt, socks, and gloves; a stick; and a bag big enough to haul everything around in. That doesn't count any registration fees, fees for league or tournament participation, or the cost of ice time.

AT A GLANCE

Salary Range

Earnings depend on the level of professional hockey. A player in the National Hockey League (NHL), the game's top level, can earn a salary worth several million dollars a year. Following the cancellation of the 2004–05 season, player salaries were cut by 24 percent as part of the labor settlement. In the American Hockey League, one level below the NHL, salaries can range from $40,000 to more than $80,000 a year. Players in any of the other, lower minor leagues, such as the East Coast Hockey League, the Central Hockey League, or the United States Hockey League, earn about $500 a week.

Experience/Education

There are no educational requirements for becoming a professional hockey player, but a college degree is recommended as something to fall back on should your dreams of a hockey career not work out.

Personal Attributes

You'll need to be hard-working, physically fit, doggedly determined, and highly motivated, because the competition for scholarships in college and roster spots at the professional level will be very keen. If you're the kind of person who is able to weather disappointments and come back even stronger, so much the better, because you're likely to endure some disappointments along the way.

Requirements

In addition to having excellent skating skills, you'll also need to be in outstanding physical condition, as hockey is a rigorous sport that requires strength, speed, stamina, and toughness.

Outlook

As with any sport, there are many more people wanting to make a professional roster than there are roster spots. Because the popularity of the game has grown considerably in the United States over the past several years, the job market figures to become even tighter, because there will be many more players than there are teams.

Children's teams often have to practice whenever ice time is available, so a workout scheduled for rather late in the evening—9, 10, or 11 o'clock—isn't unusual.

Most kids play on club teams, many of which are sanctioned by USA Hockey, the national governing body for the sport in the United States. The teams are divided

Sandy Cohen, professional hockey player

In the United States, the first sports gift a child is likely to receive is a baseball glove, a football, or a basketball. You won't find too many Canadian kids, though, getting one these. Canada is hockey country, so much so that it's practically a way of life. So when Sandy Cohen was all of 3 years old, he received his first pair of ice skates. By the time he turned 4, he was playing on a hockey team.

"I grew up in Canada where hockey is the main sport and every kid wants to be in the NHL," says Cohen, a native of Whitby, Ontario. "From an early age, hockey was more than just fun; it was a passion and I couldn't wait to get onto the ice each time."

As Cohen grew up, he played hockey on some of the top-level teams in his area, trying out against several hundred other kids. By the time he turned 15, he was playing junior hockey, which in Canada can mean moving away from home. Cohen began playing for a team in Ontario, but it wasn't long before he knew it was time for a change.

"I soon realized that I needed to move away to join a team that would give me the exposure I needed to achieve my goal of a full athletic scholarship to a Division I school in the United States," he says.

Cohen joined the Sioux City Musketeers in Sioux City, Iowa. The team was a member of the United States Hockey League (USHL), which was considered the top junior league in the country. At the time, only Americans were allowed to play in the USHL. Fortunately, Cohen had dual citizenship in Canada and the United States.

He played well enough for Sioux City to earn the college scholarship he was shooting for and got a full scholarship to Merrimack College in North Andover, Massachusetts. Cohen's college career was also a success. He graduated from Merrimack in 2000 with a degree in marketing, but his marketing career was put on hold, because he was invited to attend the training camp of the NHL's Carolina Hurricanes as a free agent.

"I had a great camp and earned a contract to play for one of their farm teams in Trenton, New Jersey," Cohen says.

He spent most of the 2000–2001 season with Trenton of the East Coast Hockey League, but at the end of the season he was traded to the Florida Everblades. Before the start of the 2001–02 season, he was traded to the Reading Royals, where he retired after one season because of a series of concussions.

A typical day for Cohen started by going to the rink at 8:30 a.m., when he and his teammates would ride the stationary bike and do some stretching exercises to loosen up. Besides getting everyone ready for practice, that time in the gym also helped the team bond.

Practice usually began at 10 and lasted for about 90 minutes, after which each player would work on individual skills. Then came a stint in the weight room and another bike ride to cool down. Because most of Cohen's games took place on the weekend, workouts were usually most intense on Mondays and Tuesdays. On game days, the schedule varied, depending on whether the game was

by age categories for boys and girls, starting at 8-and-under and continuing up to 18-and-under for boys and 19-and-under for girls. These club teams are in addition to high school teams on which young adults might play.

For the most skilled young players—those who might go on to play in

at home or on the road. But regardless of the site of the game, the workouts would be much lighter.

"It's all about routine as an athlete, especially if things are going well," Cohen explains. "If they aren't, then you look to get into a new routine that will work. You might change or tweak things slightly."

The game, which can be very rough and sometimes violent, took a physical toll on Cohen. In addition to the concussions that eventually led to his retirement, he also suffered from an assortment of bumps and bruises, some of which (sore wrist, bad back, creaky knees) still plague him to this day.

Then there were the long bus trips, too many nights in hotel rooms, and the lack of job security that made life as a hockey player stressful.

But to hear Cohen tell it, the positives far outweighed the negatives.

"The best part of being a professional hockey player was getting paid to play the sport that you love, which encompassed a few things," Cohen says. "I loved being able to perform in front of a crowd. I loved the fact that my job required me to keep my body in top physical shape. I especially liked all the 'free' stuff and having all your equipment—your skates, your custom-made sticks, your pads, your clothing, and your jersey—paid for.

"Even the media attention was pretty cool and a unique aspect of the job that I liked. I also enjoyed the fact that as long as you were playing, that dream of playing at the next level—and playing in the NHL—was still alive."

The best chance a young player has of making it to the professional level, says Cohen, is to play as much as you can at the top levels of junior hockey.

"But not everyone who plays at one of those levels is good enough to play in the ECHL," Cohen says. "You basically had to be a very solid player at those levels to make it in the pros."

Cohen says the path to a professional hockey career is a bit more difficult for American juniors than their Canadian counterparts. "If you're not recruited by an NCAA Division I program right out of high school, there's still hope," Cohen says. "The best way to still get a scholarship is to either play for a prep school, typically in New England, or, better yet, try and play for a team in the United States Hockey League or the Eastern Junior Hockey League. These two leagues are the top recruiting grounds for Division I colleges."

Cohen says you can play in those leagues while you're in high school or after you have graduated from high school. "It's up to you to play well enough to earn a college scholarship and then excel at the college level to get a look from the pro scouts," he says.

And even if things don't work out and you don't make it to the pro level, all is not lost. "You have to keep in mind that hockey isn't everything," Cohen says. "To even be able to earn a Division I scholarship, you have to make good grades. So your work in the classroom is just as important as what you do on the ice."

college or even the pros—USA Hockey has a junior program for players 20-and-under that is geared toward skill development and playing against better competition. Tier I features 16 to 20 of the best players in the country. Tier II has three classes (A, B, and C) that offer opportunities to players who don't have quite the talent or the experience to play at the top level.

USA Hockey conducts a number of festivals and player development camps each year to select players to take part in national and international competitions, including the Olympics. Boys from 14 to 17 and girls 14 to 18 are eligible.

Pitfalls

Hockey is no different than any other sport: Reaching the professional level is a long, difficult road. There are many more candidates that there are jobs, so be prepared for some disappointments along the way. If you're lucky enough to make it to the professional level, the travel can be brutal, especially in the minor leagues where most of the road trips are taken by bus.

Perks

If you've put in the time and the effort to make it as a professional hockey player, you're going to get paid for playing a game that you love, and as perks go, they don't get much better than that.

Get a Jump on the Job

Practice, practice, practice—and then practice some more. Hockey requires not only that you be in great physical shape, but also that you be able to play your sport while on skates. Work hard and try to play against the best competition that you can, because it will only make you a better player.

MINOR LEAGUE GENERAL MANAGER

OVERVIEW

Minor league sports have become big business throughout the United States over the last decade or so, with baseball and hockey leading the way. Going to a minor league game gives fans the chance to see up-and-coming young players and to have a whole lot of fun. Being the general manager of a minor league baseball or hockey team means you have to know something about sports and something about party-planning, because most minor league sports put the emphasis on entertainment every single night.

The most successfully run minor league teams rely on fun and games, in addition to the game itself. There are contests, video scoreboard displays, activities for fans between innings or periods, giveaways, fireworks, postgame concerts, and promotions, some of which can be on the wacky side.

Sports Illustrated recently cited 10 minor league baseball promotions it considered the most imaginative. One of the more bizarre examples occurred in Hagerstown, Maryland. The Hagerstown Suns held Preplanned Funeral Night. The team gave away a full, prepaid funeral, including embalming, a casket, funeral home use, and a death certificate. Sure it sounds gruesome, but more than 2,000 people entered the contest.

As you can see, a vivid imagination is essential for a successful minor league general manager.

Mike Barack, minor league hockey executive

Like a lot of kids growing up, Mike Barack's dream job was to be the play-by-play announcer for a major league team, preferably a baseball or hockey team. So after he graduated from the University of Missouri, Barack sent out resumes and audition tapes to every team in the National Hockey League and in Major League Baseball. Unfortunately, he didn't get a job with a team in either league, but he was able to land a job broadcasting for an American Hockey League team, which he did with several teams for 15 years.

"During that time, I learned all of the 'behind the scenes' workings of professional sports, including public relations, marketing, sales, broadcasting, human resources, and game set-ups," Barack says.

In July 1998, Barack made a career change. Thanks to the experience he gained through broadcasting, he accepted the job as general manager of the Fort Worth Brahmas of the Central Hockey League.

Since Barack took over, the team has increased ticket sales, corporate support, and community involvement. The Brahmas were named the league's most improved franchise in 1999 and 2000, and Barack was a co-winner of the league's executive of the year award in 2001.

"The main part of the job was my ability in sales," he says. "That was a key in getting offered a position to run the Brahmas. The ability to generate sales and revenue for a team is crucial for survival. The sales include sponsorships, tickets, and merchandise. A sports team can't operate without it."

No two days are alike as a minor league general manager. "There is no typical day," says Barack. "One day I could be on the phone all day, trying to sell some sponsorships or season tickets. Another day could be filled with dealing with our city leaders in putting together a lease or helping decide which signage pieces should go where."

Then he might stick around the arena on a game day, or spend his time traveling to a league meeting or out visiting with clients. "And some days it could be helping everyone load boxes of hats that were just delivered," he says. "The job is all encompassing; new challenges and developments take place every day. I like the opportunity to lead an organization with various challenges, such as trying to put together a winning team or gaining a new sponsor."

But besides coming up with ideas for promotions, a minor league general manager has to be to an effective salesman. He or she needs to sell tickets, team merchandise and concessions to fans, and he also has to sell his team to businesses in hopes that they will spend advertising dollars.

In order to accomplish sales goals, it's up to the general manager to oversee the marketing strategy and any public relations work necessary. In other words, other than actually playing in the game, the gen-

eral manager has a hand in just about everything that goes on with a minor league team.

As for identifying, acquiring, and assembling a team, that's something a hockey general manager has to do, but a baseball general manager doesn't.

In baseball, almost all minor league teams are affiliated with a major league team. It's the responsibility of the major league team to provide players for their minor league affiliates. There are three

What he doesn't like are employees who don't share his passion and enthusiasm for the job. In fact, he says his pet peeve is laziness, and that one of the worst business decisions an executive can make is to retain employees who aren't productive.

Barack has thrived because of his passion and enthusiasm for his job, and those characteristics have rubbed off on others in the organization, which explains the success he and the team have enjoyed during his tenure as general manager. But a positive attitude and a strong work ethic aren't the only keys to moving up the ladder in minor league sports. Barack emphasizes the importance of getting as much on the job training as possible, whether it be as an intern, a volunteer, or a part-time employee.

"Whatever it takes to work with a team from the ground up will give anyone the necessary experience to get a full-time job," Barack says. "And no matter what, learn to sell either yourself or a product. Teams are always looking to make money and people will always have a job in sports if they can prove to their employer that they can help make the team money because of their efforts.

"So no matter what, get involved, even if it is just for a game night event. Experience is the way to get a full-time position. Even if it is simply to volunteer, that would be the best way to show a potential employer your passion. And it is great for your resume, down the line.

"Lastly, by getting a chance to volunteer or become an intern, you'll get firsthand knowledge of what is expected in the sports industry and what happens off the field to put on an event."

Once you have the experience and it comes time to apply for a full-time position with a minor league team, Barack stresses the need to be persistent. Leaving your resume with a prospective employer or making a token follow-up phone call after an interview doesn't cut it. Barack says you have to call and call and continue to call until you reach the person who's doing the hiring.

When that happens, use the opportunity to make it clear why you're the right person for the job and explain the impact you'll make on the organization. Barack says you have to be "persistent almost to the point of being a nuisance." He is the same way with the people he deals with. He does whatever it takes to get people involved with the team and make the organization a success. Given his track record with the Brahmas, Barack's is a management style that works.

levels of minor league baseball—Triple A, Double A, and Single A, with Triple A being the highest. Players are assigned to teams based on their experience and ability. The minor league general manager of a baseball team has little or no say over which players are assigned to his team.

Hockey works somewhat differently. While National Hockey League teams provide some players to their minor league affiliates, many of the roster spots are filled by the minor league team itself. A minor league general manager has some input into those personnel decisions, which means he or she needs the ability to evaluate talent.

One thing that minor league baseball general managers have to deal with that their hockey counterparts don't are stadiums that feature things you wouldn't necessarily associate with a stadium. There are some stadiums that have picnic areas, food courts, a game area for kids, and even a swimming pool. Having to manage these facilities within the main stadium—and perhaps get companies to sponsor them—is just another challenge for the general manager.

Regardless of the sport and the challenges it provides, the bottom line remains the same: A minor league general manager's first and foremost goal is to make sure the fans have the best time possible. Because if they have fun once, it's a pretty safe bet they'll come back again.

Pitfalls

The hours are long, especially during the season, when 10- to 12-hour days could be the norm. You also will have to spend a lot of your time seeking new sponsors.

If you don't like being a salesman, this may not be the career for you.

Perks

You get to be around a game that you love and provide a fun, family atmosphere for your fan base. You also get a chance to be creative when it comes to developing new promotions to make the experience more enjoyable.

Get a Jump on the Job

Many minor league teams offer internships, which is a great way to develop a variety of skills. You'll also get a firsthand view of what's involved in running a team.

PERSONAL FITNESS TRAINER

OVERVIEW

It used to be that only the rich and famous had the time and the money to employ personal fitness trainers, who were considered a luxury and limited to the Hollywood starlet worried about her figure or the rugged leading man wanting to improve his physique.

But that was then. Now, thanks to the proliferation of health clubs throughout the United States and the increased awareness of physical fitness, having a personal trainer isn't just for the red carpet crowd. People from all walks of life are making the commitment to good health by working out with a personal trainer. Many of those people are children, brought to personal trainers by their parents, who want to give them every opportunity to excel in sports and perhaps earn a college scholarship.

The first step in becoming a successful personal trainer is to get yourself in top physical condition. Clients want to hire a personal trainer who's in excellent shape.

But looks aren't everything. You can have the best build since Arnold Schwarzenegger in his prime, but if you don't have the knowledge, the experience, and the personality to make your clients happy, then your career will be short lived.

A bachelor's degree isn't required, and you could do just fine without one—but a recent study revealed that the most knowledgeable personal trainers also happen to be better educated. Here's something else to keep in mind: Some organizations,

AT A GLANCE

Salary Range

The average hourly rate for a personal fitness trainer is about $50, but rates can range as low as $15 an hour and as high as $100, depending on where you live. For example, a personal trainer in an urban setting is likely to charge a lot more than one in a more rural setting.

Education/Experience

While you can become a successful personal trainer without earning a bachelor's degree, having a degree on your wall won't hurt. If you decide a degree is the way to go, your best bets are exercise science, exercise physiology, sports medicine, physical education, biomechanics (the study of applying mechanical principles to how the human body works), or kinesiology (the study of muscles and muscular movement).

Personal Attributes

You should be in great physical shape and be upbeat, enthusiastic, encouraging, and patient. Being able to motivate your clients to do one more rep or run another lap around the track will come in handy, as well.

Requirements

You absolutely, positively have to be certified by a nationally recognized organization, and there are a slew of organizations out there that certify trainers. Be sure you're certified by one that's reputable, such as the American College of Sports Medicine (ACSM), the National Strength and Conditioning Association (NSCA), or the American Council on Exercise (ACE). Certifications generally last for two years, after which you have to be recertified by attending continuing education classes.

Outlook

Excellent. We live in a society in which fit, trim, and toned is all the rage. Notice all the infomercials on television promising six-pack abs and rippling muscles. People are spending more time and money on fitness, and so are many businesses, which have instituted wellness programs in order to reduce their insurance costs. Personal trainers should see an increase in demand for their services.

Aaron M. Potts, personal trainer

It was the late 1990s, the stock market was flourishing, and life was good for Aaron Potts. He worked for InfoSpace, a company that was involved in mobile technology and Internet search engines. His job was high-paying and not very difficult, he says. InfoSpace was very successful; its stock traded as high as $250 per share.

But by late in 2000, the dot-com bubble burst, and the price of InfoSpace stock sunk like a stone. Suddenly, the financial security and the benefits that Potts enjoyed had disappeared. He was at a crossroads, trying to weigh his options for the future.

"When everything came to a screeching halt, I decided to make my move," he says. Potts relocated from the West Coast to Jacksonville, Florida, where he began to work as a personal fitness trainer.

"Going out on my own was a very big risk," he says. "I had some money in the bank that I lived off of, but I was also doing a full career change, which meant that I had to basically learn how to 'work' all over again. That was radically time consuming, especially since I tried several different avenues before deciding on in-home personal training.

"Also during this time the horrific events of 9-11 happened, and I had to struggle through a very tough economy, as well as a nation more occupied with life, death, and foreign affairs than physical fitness."

But after a lot of hard work, patience, and dedication, Potts has established himself as a successful personal trainer. One of the main reasons he's successful is that he "teaches" his clients how to work out properly, instead of just "demonstrating."

"Just because you are good at working out, does not mean you will be a good personal trainer," Potts says. "Anyone can show someone how to do a bicep curl or a lunge. You can pick up a magazine and learn that. The key component missing is actual teachers, not just trainers."

So Potts makes teaching a priority, and he also makes sure he keeps up with the changes in the industry by doing research and constantly educating himself. The key is to be able to adapt your

such as the American Council on Exercise (ACE), won't certify a trainer without a formal degree in exercise science or a related field.

You'll also need to be certified by a recognized, reputable organization. Be aware that only half of the 400 organizations that certify trainers in the United States are considered to be legitimate.

You should also add CPR training and liability insurance to your list. If you work for a fitness center or health club, you're probably covered by your employer; but if you're an independent contractor, you'll have to take care of it yourself.

Many personal fitness trainers work individually with their clients, either in the client's home or the trainer's studio, so be prepared to work long hours to fit your clients' schedules. This is not necessarily a 9-to-5 job, and if you try to turn it into one, your clients will most likely get another trainer who's more flexible.

Once you have a customer base, your task is to motivate your clients and whip them into shape. Depending on the personalities you're dealing with, you could be re-teaching style and technique to the wide variety of clients you serve. Not every person has the same fitness goal, so it's up to the personal trainer to be able to provide what each client wants.

Potts sees most of his clients in their homes, so he has to be available when they are. That can mean long days, lots of travel, and a schedule that changes constantly.

"A typical day for me is hectic, but that's a good thing," Potts says. "I've had days that started as early as 4 a.m. and ended as late as 11 p.m. I've had days with back-to-back clients for more than 12 hours straight, and I've had days where I only had one training appointment.

"No two days are ever the same when you are a personal fitness trainer. What matters more than the content of 'a day in the life of a personal trainer,' is the 'life in the day of a personal trainer.' I surround myself with fitness and fitness-related endeavors, and every day is a brand new adventure."

Unfortunately for Potts, each day only has 24 hours in it, which means he can only help a certain number of people each day. "That's the thing I like least about my job," he says.

What he likes best is that every day "has more positive in it than negative," Potts says. "I'm not going to lie and say every day is a piece of cake, and I run around grinning from ear to ear because my life is so easy and grand. However, every single day, without fail, has more positive in it than negative."

If you think you'd like to become a personal fitness trainer, Potts recommends that you be motivated, that you be prepared to work hard, and that you genuinely enjoy people.

"If you are considering a career in the fitness industry," Potts says, "you should ask yourself, 'Why?' If your motivation is financial freedom, social status, easy workdays, or any similar reasons, don't bother.

"Being a fitness professional requires dedication, commitment, and above all, the ability to truly care about people. Don't just say you care about people—mean it. If you don't, you'll find yourself back at square one, looking for a new career. However, if you truly care about people, then the fitness industry is for you."

quired to do a bit of drill sergeant work with some and more cheerleading with others. That's why it's important to be a people person. It also helps to be very clear on what each client wants to achieve. Everyone has different goals, and it's up to you to tailor your workouts on an individual basis.

But there's more to your job than simply focusing on how many reps your clients do and how much weight they lift. A really outstanding trainer will also preach the benefits of a healthy lifestyle. In other words, the road to fitness includes more than the weekly session with the trainer.

Being healthy means eating right, getting plenty of rest, and minimizing your intake of alcohol.

The schedule of a personal fitness trainer can tend to be hectic because you have to be available when your clients are. That could mean early starts and late finishes. If you have to travel to work with your clients, you'll have an even longer day, not to mention travel expenses.

Perks

The satisfaction you'll get knowing you've helped someone improve his or her quality of life is one of the main reasons personal trainers are so enthusiastic about their jobs.

Get a Jump on the Job

Being in shape is a prerequisite. It's also important to understand as much as you can about the different aspects of training, such as weightlifting and cardiovascular workouts. Working with a variety of trainers will also give you some insight into the styles and methods used.

PIT CREW MEMBER

OVERVIEW

If you've ever watched a car race on TV, you've probably seen the pit crew fly into action. The car races in, six guys descend on the car like a horde of locusts—as tires spin, fuel flows, and lug nuts fly—and in about 10 seconds the car is back on the race track, all ready to go for another 120 laps.

A typical pit stop begins three laps before the car enters pit lane, as the team discusses how they want to handle the pit stop. Typically, a stop includes changing four tires, refueling, and making wing and tire pressure adjustments. To be successful, the pit crew must make sure that the right tools are available. Typically, a race team will designate one or two crew members to set up the pits so the tires and tools are all in place. The pit crew then steps over the wall and waits for the car, secure in the knowledge that everything that could possibly be done before the car arrives is already taken care of.

The car comes in, the pit crew jumps into action, and the car then takes off and continues the race. During the pit stop, the videotape is running so the staff can study it later. During the tape review, pit crew members note who hesitated, how long, and why, and try to make sure it doesn't happen again. Everyone is encouraged to offer suggestions at the crew's weekly meeting.

Pit crews may be large or small, depending on how much money a racing

AT A GLANCE

Salary Range

When traveling to a race, pit crew members receive a per diem and paid hotel accommodations. Their salary is based on performance, although it's difficult to determine what an average salary would be. If the race car wins, the entire team (including the pit crew) shares in the winnings.

Education/Experience

Pit crew members come from all walks of life and all educational backgrounds. No degree is required, but obviously the more hands-on mechanical experience you can get, the better. One thing all pit crew members have in common is a love of cars and racing.

Personal Attributes

An ideal pit crew member is a team player who thrives on competition and who can remain focused under extreme pressure. You also have to be quite strong and fairly young, to handle this very physical job. Size isn't important; catch can guys are usually taller because they need to be able to reach the track bar to make adjustments. Tire carriers need to be stocky and are often shorter, and tire changers are typically shorter and more flexible.

Requirements

Consistency, ability to work hard and maintain top performance. Most pit crew members are men, but there are a few women.

Outlook

Excellent. The popularity of motor sports (especially NASCAR) is growing by leaps and bounds, which should only increase the available number of pit crew jobs.

team has, but the actual pit crew includes just those individuals who service the car during a pit stop. Different racing organizations have different rules for how many people can be working in the pit at any one time. For example, NASCAR allows only seven individuals in the pit servicing a car at any one time during a pit stop.

A typical active pit crew is typically composed of the front tire changer, the rear tire changer, the jack man, the gas catch man, and the tire carriers (there may be two of these). The front tire changer is responsible for changing the right and left front tires, and likewise, the rear tire changer changes the right and left rear tires. The tire changers also make any necessary changes to the tire mounts.

The jack man (sometimes called the leader of the pit stop) is responsible for jacking the car up so the tire changers can replace the tires. The faster the jack man works, the quicker the tires are changed, and the faster the car can be on its way. The jack man uses a powerful, light rolling jack to move the car up quickly with the least amount of effort. Once the right side is done, he moves over to the left, and as soon as he drops the car, the driver takes off.

Gas is an important part of a pit stop, and the gas man uses a special gas can equipped with a customized valve that easily fits into the car's gas port to fill the tank quickly. A full gas can weighs up to 90 pounds, and it usually takes two of them to fill the tank.

If any fuel overflows, the extra is the responsibility of the gas catch man, who applies a special "catch can" to the car's gasoline overflow vent to gather up any gas that flows back from a full tank. The gas catch man also may be responsible for holding the second full gas can on his shoulder.

There are usually two tire carriers (one for the front and one for the back of the car), who run up with new replace-ment tires and help guide them correctly onto the lugs. The front tire carrier also may be required to clean the grille. Depending on the race car team, there may be many other members working in the pit crew. Some may stand by to give the driver a drink, wash the windshield, help the tire changers and carriers, fill gas cans, or hold the pit board, a sign used to help the driver determine exactly where his pit stall is.

The job may sound straightforward—but try doing any of these tasks during a race, when every second counts and you know you're being videotaped for later review of your performance. It's quite possible that a mistake by any one of the pit crew members could mean the loss of a race, and thousands of dollars down the drain.

Time is of utmost importance. It takes about six seconds to change a tire. (One way that's possible is that racing cars use only one lug nut in the middle, as compared to five on a regular car.) And it takes about 10 to 12 seconds to fuel the car. The crew will typically aim to get the whole job done in less than 11 seconds. The key here is consistency. You're aiming not just to get the job done and done right—but done in just a few seconds under adverse conditions.

Typically, a race team will practice three times a week, either performing drills or practicing, with each pit crew member putting in from 15 to 20 hours a week in training and practicing. You have to be strong to carry tires and perform other roles. It's rigorous work, and the young-er you are, the better. Pit crew members should be in their early- to mid-20s. Once you enter your 30s, you'll probably have to make adjustments in your job if you want to remain a part of a pit crew, such

Chad Kendrick, pit crew member

Ever since he was a boy, Chad Kendrick has dreamt of car racing. "My family has always been involved in racing, in one form or another," he says. "I started racing go-karts, and I've always either raced or been involved in race cars."

Today, he's the jackman for Bobby Hamilton's NASCAR Craftsman truck series. "I'm the first one over the wall [during a pit stop], and I get to the race car as quick as I can," he explains. It's the jack man who starts and ends the pit stop. As the truck comes in, the jack man runs to the right side and slides the jack under the passenger side, jacking it up with a lightweight aluminum jack. "We use a one-pump jack," Kendrick says, "it's not as much muscle as weight transfer." Once the truck is up, the jack man must make sure it stays stable and that loose tires don't knock the jack out. Once the right side is finished, the jackman runs to the left side and does the same thing. Once service is complete, Kendrick releases the jack, letting the truck drop to the ground. That's the driver's signal that he can leave the pit stall. Kendrick does it all—from jumping over the wall to the finished job— in between five and six seconds.

"It was always something I wanted to do," he explains. A former high school football player and athlete, he says he likes doing anything athletic—and being a jackman is certainly a physical job. Of course, like almost all pit crew members and everyone else working at the track, in his heart he'd love to be racing. "I enjoy both [racing and working in the crew]," Kendrick says. "A lot of people's goal is to be a race car driver, but there are only 43 drivers. For all those who can't be behind the wheel, the next best thing is being a pit crew member. But I guess in the back of all our minds is the dream of racing."

It's not always an easy life, especially for pit crew members who are married and have a family, because there's so much travel involved. Kendrick says he's on the road 30 to 40 weekends a year. "Travel can get strenuous," he says. "Maybe there are 12 or 15 weeks a year you don't travel out of town." Kendrick, who's single and doesn't have kids, says it doesn't really bother him that much. "But I can see if I was married, it would be more of a problem."

He loves the friendships he has with the other crew members and the drivers. "The camaraderie you build with the guys—they are all the people I hang out with. Even if I wasn't going to a race, I spend time with the people at the shop. We're together until 10 or 11 at night, we're on the road together—you don't have a choice but to like each other! We have real tight friendships with the crew and drivers."

If you love the racing world, NASCAR, and cars or trucks in general, it pays to get as much experience as you can, Kendrick says. Within the past five years, he's seen the sport become much more competitive, not just for the drivers, but for everyone on the team, including the mechanics and the pit crew. There are now schools to learn how to work on a pit crew, although Kendrick doesn't know enough about those programs to recommend them or not. "I went to college, although not for this," he says. He'd recommend that if you're interested in racing, you get involved in any way you can. "Help out at a local track, learn as much as you can, starting with the most basic things—[such as] how to put on a lug nut. Help people out, learn as much as you can. Eventually, someone may give you a break and start you on your way to a race team career."

For now, for him, it's the perfect job. "I never wake up say: 'Durn! I have to go to work!' Every day I wake up and say I'm glad I'm doing what I want to be doing."

as moving to catch can, which isn't as physically strenuous.

If you want to get a job in a pit crew and a family member isn't on the race team, it helps to be in the right place at the right time. Jobs are typically landed via word of mouth. Some teams have in-training individuals who may travel with the team.

Pitfalls

It's tough to have a family life and work on a pit crew because your hours are long and unpredictable, and during the racing season you'll be away from home traveling across the country for weeks at a time. It's also a tough, demanding, physically exhausting, and mentally stressful occupation.

Perks

For the pit crew members on a race car team, nothing is more rewarding than helping to service a fast car that's capable of winning races. When that car does win, you not only get the satisfaction of knowing your hard work and long hours were worth it—you also get a piece of the financial bonus.

Get a Jump on the Job

You're not likely to be hired on a pit crew in high school, but you can spend this time visiting races, visiting the pits before the races, and reading everything you can about car racing. If you're interested in cars, take auto mechanics courses in school or attend an auto racing school.

RACEHORSE GROOM

OVERVIEW

No matter how much you like horses, if you're not good at getting up at the crack of dawn, the job of racehorse groom isn't for you. Typically, grooms report to work at about 4:30 a.m. in time to clean out stalls and check the condition of the stalls first clues to the horses' health. You're also expected to keep an eye out for any injuries, unusual behavior, lack of appetite, and so on.

Feeding comes next—an important chore for any horse, but particularly so for racehorses. Grooms must understand different types of feed and be aware of the symptoms of colic and how to respond. Then comes grooming, including giving wet and dry baths, checking and cleaning the hooves, applying fly spray, and a mud knot in the tail. The techniques of cooling a horse properly after exercise are also important, along with understanding the issues of safe transport, including how to properly bandage the legs and load horses into a van.

It's not just the mechanics that you have to know. The rapport between groom and horse is critical. Trainers are convinced that a happy horse is a faster horse, and grooms play a vital role in keeping their horses happy. In the high-stakes world of horse racing, whatever makes the horse happy makes the trainer and owner happy. That's why grooms are traditionally sent along with racehorses when they are shipped to other tracks for big races.

In addition to feeding and grooming, grooms typically lead the racehorses from the barn to the saddling ring to keep the skittish animals calm while thousands of fans may be screaming. For an animal that can spook by a piece of paper fluttering by in the wind, keeping calm at a racetrack is no small feat.

Pitfalls

Horses are huge, powerful animals just waiting to bite, kick, or trample anyone perceived as a threat, and thoroughbred racehorses are some of the touchiest of all—especially the stallions. Grooms face a real risk of injury, long hours, and low earnings (take-home pay averages about $375 a week). They

Lenny Gomer, racehorse groom

For 30 years, Philadelphia Park in Bensalem, Pennsylvania, has been home to Lenny Gomer, racehorse groom. "I used to go to the track when I was a teenager," he says, "and I thought if I got a job there, I'd know who was gonna win. I quickly found out that's not the way it works!"

The work can be hard, itinerant, poorly paid, sometimes dangerous, and most people do it because they love it. Gomer has been there ever since his first teenage job at the track. "It's nice to be outdoors," he explains. "It's not the same thing every day. Your horses change, and it's a lot of fun. It's interesting!"

At Philly Park, 36 long, plain barns house about 1,200 horses. On his first day on the job, Gomer didn't know much of anything about horses, so he started out as a hotwalker—the person who walks the racehorse after he's been running, until he's cool enough to safely eat and drink without risking colic, a potentially fatal intestinal cramping. It's not an easy job—you're walking around hanging onto a lead attached to a 1,500-pound thoroughbred not known for being calm and peaceful. Many of these racehorses spook easily. Thoroughbreds are bred to be aggressive, and all it takes is a bit of paper flapping by that they see out of the corner of their eye, and they'll knock you down without thinking.

Eventually, as time went on, Gomer learned more about horses and became a groom. Some grooms dream of moving on to exercise boy, maybe to jockey, maybe to trainer.

After six months of hotwalking, Gomer had learned enough to start working for one trainer, getting his own four horses to care for. "As a groom, you do a little bit of everything," Gomer explains. On a typical day, he'll muck out the stalls, brush the horses, and get them ready to go to the track. When they come back from their workout or race, the grooms bathe them, washing off the dirt from the track. In order to keep horses calm during the bath, he'll run a chain under the top lip, over the gum, where there's a pressure point. Then the grooms usually apply a poultice, which helps draw heat from their legs. Some grooms use mud, and others stuff ice into leg vests; sometimes cayenne is applied to the outside of the bandages, to keep horses from chewing them off. Then it's time to get the horse his lunch.

It's tough, dirty work that can be physically exhausting. "When I first came on the racetrack, all the trainers were men and all the grooms were men," he says. "Now there are some women trainers and about half the grooms are women." Even for people who love horses, being a racehorse groom is rough. Working at the track isn't like a traditional job; your busiest days are often weekends and holidays. Gomer typically works lots of hours, seven days a week. He'll usually take one day a week off. He admits it's no walk in the park, either. Working around horses is a very dangerous job, handling high-strung animals who seem ready to fly apart at a moment's notice. Broken bones are not at all unusual around the track; grooms have been kicked and trampled on—but it's just considered part of the game.

Thirty years ago, Gomer says he sort of fell into his job as a groom. Today, the best way to get started in a job working with horses at a track is by asking everyone and anyone you know in the horse world whether they need help. It could mean mucking stalls for a few hours a day at one barn, riding horses that need a workout, or spending night shifts on the foal watch in the spring and early summer.

If you're not small enough or brave enough to be a jockey, you might consider working at a racing stable as a groom. Gomer admits he's sorry he didn't go on to stay in school, but nevertheless, he does enjoy working with animals in the outdoors. "I'm not married, so it's a good job for me. But if you have a family, it might be harder to pay the bills."

typically sleep in a nearby dormitory room barely bigger than one of the stalls.

Perks

If you love and understand horses and racing, you'll be willing to put up with almost anything in order to work with these intelligent, beautiful animals. The job of racing groom appeals to those who love horses, freedom, and the outdoors, those who wouldn't be happy chained to a desk job and who appreciate the responsibility they are given for these creatures.

Get a Jump on the Job

You can start getting involved with horses and ponies almost as soon as you can toddle around, if there's someone who will put you on the back of a mount. Take horseback riding lessons as early as you can, and hang around in the stables. Offer to help muck out for free to get used to being around the animals, or attend a horseback riding camp to learn. The more information you can soak up about horses, the better able to handle them you'll get. If you're not able to buy your own horse when you get older, you can still help out in horse camps or stables.

SCOREBOARD OPERATOR

OVERVIEW

In the old days, you'd be lucky to figure out the basic score on the hand-lettered, manually operated boards tacked up across the field, where operators slid wooden block numbers in and out of slots. Today, fans are treated to a complex, computerized extravaganza of statistics and information. If you're sitting at a baseball game, for example, on the scoreboard you'll see pictures of the batter, his batting history, instant replays, plus information about other games in the majors that night—in addition to the scores, RBIs, errors, outs, strikes, and other statistics. There might be some snazzy ads, some interesting crowd shots, and lots of music.

It's the job of the scoreboard operator to run the scoreboard that displays game statistics and ads, and it's big business. The New York Yankees' main scoreboard, for example, is more than 500 feet long, and 11 people work on their scoreboard team.

A ballpark scoreboard in the early 20th century was a simple device that got the job done—and that's about it. Typically, the boards only provided information about the game being played. For example, a baseball scoreboard listed the home team and visitor, with nine squares in a vertical line. With the onset of electricity came huge electric scoreboards that added all kinds of information sports fanatics were dying to have—team names, lineups, cumulative total of runs or touchdowns. Some of the big league scoreboards began

providing a list of all the other games in progress in the majors that day, along with their scores. Numbers and letters flashed out on a black background.

Today's scoreboards are a breed apart—computer-operated, 100-foot wide hi-definition screens that blur the line between traditional stadium scoreboards and broadcast-quality television video production. These boards—and the operators who run them—have revolutionized the stadium experience with a combination of high-quality video, timely information, exciting animations, and custom graphics.

Kyle Ritchie, scoreboard operator

Ever since he was in college at James Madison University, Kyle Ritchie was out there on the sidelines, videotaping basketball and football games, editing the footage, doing coaches shows, and capturing the action of his college teams. Today, he's the director of entertainment for the Carolina Panthers, with responsibility for the entire scoreboard operation. "The videoboard, the clocks, showing the actual scores, downs, distance—all of that falls under us," he says. "If something goes wrong with the videoboard, I'm the guy who they call."

For the past 18 years, Kyle Ritchie has been "the guy they call" when it comes to scoreboards and stadium entertainment—first with the Baltimore Orioles right out of college, and then with the Miami Dolphins and the Florida Marlins. For the past 10 years, he's been manning the booth at the Bank of America stadium in Charlotte, North Carolina, home of the NFL football team the Carolina Panthers. Ritchie is responsible for all of the entertainment displays: Both end zones are equipped with a scoreboard featuring on-scoreboard animations and replays, designed to be visible from any seat in the stadium. Each scoreboard contains a TV-quality color video board, a black-and-white matrix board with animation and game-in-progress statistics, four advertising displays, a color Tri-Vision advertising display, a clock, and a speaker cluster with more color ads. On each sideline is a board with a game clock, a logo panel, two black-and-white matrix boards displaying game-in-progress information and NFL scores, and eight ad displays. In the center of each end zone is an end zone board with a delay-of-game clock, two ad displays, and two logo panels. The stadium sound system features a central speaker cluster located on the top end of the west end zone scoreboard. Any areas that don't receive sound directly from this source receive sound from an additional speaker system with computer-timed output to reduce the impression of delay. All internal spaces, concourses, toilet facilities, club lounges, and suites have a separate speaker system.

It's all state of the art, and it's all highly computerized. This winter, the stadium is installing new sideline LED boards.

"The job has changed drastically in the 18 years I've been doing it," he says. "It's so different now, and it involves much more than it used to." All of the graphics, tie-ins to sponsors, and entertainment coordination are Kyle Ritchie's job. "If you do your job right, when you get to game day you just move through the day," he says. It's like preparation for a play—you spend months of time preparing so you can walk out on the stage and put on a flawless performance. "Basically, game day is a five-hour live TV show," he says. "You entertain the fans when the game's not going on, and you ride the flow of the game. You react to the game, but you don't take away from the game—never forget, it's football first." This means if the team is winning, you might handle the crowd and the entertainment differently than if the team is losing.

On game day, Ritchie shows up at 8 a.m. to meet with his staff; he's responsible for about 45 employees. "We do everything, from working the video screens, the sound system, the P.A. announcements, coordinate with cheerleaders, do all the pregame and halftime elements."

The scoreboard operators sit amidst a bank of computers in a small booth (usually in or near the press box), controlling the board that flashes the score and details about the game (such as the down or distance in football, or the innings and RBIs in baseball), along with information about pitching, batting, lineup, defense, and

If you love sports, computers, high-tech video equipment—this might be the career for you. "The most important thing is to love whatever sport you're working in," Ritchie says. "Everyone working in the industry are fans first. I worked baseball for eight years, and if you don't like baseball, you'll go crazy," he says. "And you've got to know the sport you're covering. Personally, I like football better, because there are fewer games," he says (about 10 to 15, compared to about 80 for baseball). "As long as you like the sport and understand it, pretty much you can find your niche.

"You need a heavy background in TV production, radio, film, or sports management," Ritchie says. "A couple of schools do specialize in the sports industry. A lot of schools offer 'sports management' as a major. They prepare people for all different jobs in the sports industry." Ritchie hires lots of grads from the broadcasting trade schools. "They get broadcasting experience, and if they're interested in sports, we take them."

When you're looking for a job as a scoreboard operator, the number one thing that should be on your resume is experience. "I did practicums, internships, hands-on work," Ritchie says. "That way, you get to know the job. That's how lots of people get into this. I've had a great stretch of interns, and almost all of them are working in the sports business."

For Ritchie, the job is a dream come true. "I like the live aspect of this job," he says. "It's happening and you have to react to it. You do a TV show, you can sit there and pick at it and try to get it just perfect. But I like the live aspect, where you're under pressure to get it down and move on." The fact that every day is different is another big plus, he says. "I enjoy the ebb and flow of being with the team, the wins and losses, players coming and going. I couldn't sit at a desk job where one week isn't different from the week before. Here, things are constantly changing, and that keeps it interesting."

Although the football season lasts for just a few months, Ritchie is busy all year long, either coping with the current season or lining up entertainment and scoreboard details for the next. When he's not working a home game during the season, he's arranging private parties and corporate events, doing cleanup, budgeting, working with the marketing department to help new sponsors get their message out. Typically, there's at least one big project each season having to do with revamping the equipment. "This year, we're installing new large sideline LED boards—they're basically long thin video screens. It's a whole new way of displaying content, and we have to learn all about them. Usually every off-season, there's something like that. It's definitely more of a 9-to-5 job during off-season, but the hours are a lot longer in the fall. "We get the busiest in early July, through August. We work day and night. We start playing games in August, so getting ready for those games takes time."

There's nothing about the job he doesn't like. "Everybody wants your job," he laughs. "There are some unglamorous aspects, but the ownership is like a family, they're wonderful. The weather is great, the team does well, and it's great to work with the team."

scores of other games played outside the league.

But the operator isn't just concerned with getting the right score up there. Score-board operators also typically have at least one—and sometimes as many as six or seven—cameras that can be deployed to capture crowd shots and instant replays.

If things are getting slow, the operator can turn to clips of sports movies and brief, animated features, or they can plug in ads from sponsors.

Pitfalls

The job can be stressful if malfunctions on the board affect play or the fans' enjoyment of the game. In smaller parks, salary isn't great and equipment lags behind that of the larger stadiums.

Perks

If you're a bit of a computer geek, love sports, and can juggle duties, this job could be a great fit. It will put you in the center of the action—and you'll have front row seats at the game every night.

Get a Jump on the Job

If you love sports, it's probably not much of a hardship to be out there at the games, learning the ropes. Take as much math and computer science as you can in school. Contact a smaller stadium in your area to see if you can help the scoreboard operator for a few games.

SNOWBOARD INSTRUCTOR

OVERVIEW

Snowboarding is a sport for fun-lovers, thrill-seekers, and daredevils. If you're not the adventurous type, save yourself the energy of climbing up the mountain and even thinking about snowboarding, which is a combination of skateboarding and surfing.

Developed in the 1960s, snowboarding has surged in popularity over the last decade or so, thanks to the annual Winter X Games, and its inclusion as an Olympic sport at the 1998 Winter Games.

Teaching snowboarding appears to be a field with lots of opportunities, especially when you consider that snowboarders already account for between 20 and 25 percent of visitors to U.S. ski resorts. Even better news for would-be instructors is a projection that by 2015, snowboarding is expected to be more popular than skiing.

However, being a snowboard instructor requires a few prerequisites, not the least of which is fearlessness. A good instructor must be able to demonstrate the moves and techniques required. The ability to communicate effectively shouldn't be underestimated, either. Explaining the do's, don'ts, and how-to's of the sport in clear, concise terms will go a long way toward your students' improvement.

It's important that you be enthusiastic, encouraging, and patient, especially when dealing with novices and children, who will no doubt need all the help they can get. A good sense of humor also comes in handy.

AT A GLANCE

Salary Range

A first-year instructor can expect to earn between $6.50 and $10 per hour for a lesson. With additional experience the fee could exceed $20 per hour. Some instructors receive tips from their students, but it's best not to count on them. An experienced and diligent snowboard instructor could make as much as $150 to $400 a day at a large upscale resort.

Education/Experience

Proficiency in snowboarding is a must. In addition to being able to handle yourself on the slopes, it's a good idea to take an instructor training course, such as the one offered by the American Association of Snowboard Instructors. The ability to communicate is also paramount to becoming a successful instructor. You have to be able to verbalize instructions and techniques in ways that students can grasp.

Personal Attributes

A positive, friendly personality is very important. You not only have to be able to explain the technical nature of snowboarding to your students, you'll also have to possess outstanding people skills. You will be working in a service-oriented industry, which means your students will have to like you, not just your instruction methods.

Requirements

Snowboard instructors should be certified by organizations such as the American Association of Snowboard Instructors or the Professional Ski Instructors of America. Being affiliated with the AASI or PSIA will give you increased credibility when you apply for a job.

Outlook

Excellent. Snowboarding continues to be one of the fastest-growing sports in the United States. While the number of skiers in the United States has declined by about 25 percent, the number of snowboarders has increased by 77 percent.

Kevin "KC" Gandee, snowboard instructor

KC Gandee grew up in the Washington, D.C., area, which is not exactly a hotbed for winter sports, unless you count navigating through the ice and snow and slow-moving traffic. But in 1989 when his father married a skier, the family started traveling to West Virginia four or five times each winter.

Gandee, who was 12 at the time, would've tried skiing, but his father suggested snowboarding because the price of snowboards was quite a bit less than skis.

His first day on the mountain was about what you'd expect: a combination of awesome and terrible at the same time. "I spent all day falling down the learner trail," he says. "Then I finally made a turn and stopped under control at the end. That one turn hooked me on the sport, despite the fact that my knees and rear end were black and blue from the falls."

Gandee's interest in snowboarding grew. He loved the sport so much that in 1996, during his second year at James Madison University in Harrisonburg, Virginia, he applied for a job as a ski lift attendant at Massanutten Resort to get the free season pass for the slopes that went with it.

Unfortunately, he didn't get the job as a lift attendant. Instead, he was asked to be an instructor. After he went through an interview, the next step was a test of his snowboarding and communication skills.

"I was so nervous on the way to that tryout that I had to pull over on the way and say goodbye to my breakfast," Gandee says. "Needless to say I made the cut at tryouts. What I didn't expect was how much fun the job could be. I was helping other people learn the sport I loved, without the pain that I had felt. It was also great to be outside all the time, interacting with people of all ages."

It wasn't long before Gandee made the decision to turn his part-time job into a full-time career. In 1998, he decided to put his college education on hold and learn all he could about snowboarding. Gandee eventually returned to school and earned a degree in management and organizational development from Eastern Mennonite University, also in Harrisonburg.

But taking the plunge and going gung-ho after a career in snowboarding paid off. Gandee became a member of the American Association of Snowboard Instructors (AASI) education staff, which meant he trained and certified other instructors on the East Coast. He also was named as one of the six members of the AASI national team, requiring him to travel throughout the United States giving clinics.

The most significant prerequisite to becoming a successful snowboard instructor is a genuine desire to work with people and help them get better. A study by the National Ski Areas Association showed that skiers and snowboarders who took lessons "were generally very enthusiastic about continuing with the sport in general and taking lessons." More than 80 per-cent of those polled said they'd continue the sport and more than 70 percent said they would continue taking lessons. So the more effective the instructor, the busier he or she will be.

Remember, most students won't have lofty aspirations of becoming a Winter X Games star or an Olympic champion. They mainly just want to have fun, learn

When he's not jetting around the country, Gandee teaches at Stratton Mountain Resort in Stratton, Vermont. A typical day starts early. He gets up at 6 a.m., eats a hearty breakfast—a must before battling the cold —and then heads to the slopes. His attire includes shin guards, rear end and hip padding, and wrist guards, because even though he's an experienced instructor, he'd rather be safe than sorry. He gives his snowboard a once over, checking that the screws are tight and the edges are sharp. Then it's on with his helmet and goggles, and at 8:30 a.m., he and his fellow instructors ride together on their snowboards to check the snow conditions.

While they're riding, they also discuss learning and teaching styles, kinesiology, equipment design, and other technical info that they can use to help people learn faster.

With the slopes checked out and the game plan in place, Gandee heads out to meet his students. "Since I have been teaching for a pretty long time, I usually have private lessons waiting for me," he says. "Private lessons are usually one-on-one lessons, but occasionally will be families or groups of friends. Many of these private lessons are with people that I have worked with before. These lessons are a lot of fun since I get to see riders progress from those first awkward days to being a smooth snowboarder." The other benefit of private lessons is that they pay more. When Gandee began as an instructor, he made $6.50 an hour. As a full-time instructor, his rate jumped to $10 an hour. Because of his experience, he can make between $150 and $400 a day teaching "private-request lessons" —which means he's hired by one client for an entire day.

When working for the AASI, Gandee earns $150 a day, plus meals, travel, and expenses. He makes additional cash by writing articles and taking pictures for magazines.

Gandee's lessons usually end around 3:30 p.m., which leaves a half-hour to go riding before the lifts close at 4 p.m. After a snowshoe walk with his dog Virginia, and a big meal, he hits the sack by 10 p.m. Eight hours of sleep is a must. But to hear Gandee tell it, the next day on the slopes can't come fast enough.

"Without a doubt, getting paid to snowboard is the best part of the job," he says. "Another favorite part of my job is watching someone nail a new trick or seeing their faces light up when they finally carve a turn for the first time. Helping others is truly a rewarding experience.

"Being an instructor can be a great career for people who like being outside and meeting and helping all types of people. There will be tough days, but if you apply yourself to learning more about teaching and riding the great days will far outnumber the difficult ones."

how to snowboard and be able to make it down the mountain without having to call 911 on the way. So instructors shouldn't get overly technical unless their students want that type of detailed lesson.

One thing that instructors have to keep in mind is that they're working in an industry that is heavily dependent on the weather. Most ski resorts pay by the hour, so if Mother Nature doesn't cooperate with weather conditions suitable to giving lessons, you could find yourself a little short in the paycheck at week's end. But as long as the weather is cold and the snow is plentiful—either man-made or the real thing—expect to teach between four and eight hours a day and be worn out when you finally hit the sack.

Pitfalls

Instructors face long days and work for fees that aren't going to make them rich, at least not right away. Weather that doesn't lend itself to snowboarding can result in instructors being laid off. Layoffs also take place as the skiing and snowboarding season comes to a close. In the summer instructors either have to find other jobs or travel to countries in the southern hemisphere, such as New Zealand, where winter is just beginning.

Perks

Far and away, the number-one benefit to being a snowboard instructor is being able to snowboard. Many instructors get into the business not just to help others improve, but to improve themselves. Working at a ski resort with beautiful surroundings and breathtaking mountain vistas isn't such a bad deal, either.

Get a Jump on the Job

Practice, practice, practice. The more proficient you can become as a snowboarder, the better chance you'll have to become an instructor. The American Association of Snowboard Instructors offers courses on a regional basis. Enrolling in one of those courses will give you an idea of what's expected from instructors, the different methods used in teaching, and how drills and games can be used to get your ideas across effectively.

SPORTS AGENT

OVERVIEW

Some people want to work as a sports agent for the chance to hang around athletes and big-time sporting events. For others, it's the chance to earn big, fat commissions as payment for negotiating contracts and lining up endorsement deals. But before a sports agent gets to represent the rich and famous athletes who are going to generate the big bucks, he or she has to climb the ladder and pay some dues.

Becoming a super sports agent—the kind quoted in the newspaper or who show up on ESPN's *SportsCenter*—doesn't happen overnight. Like all good things, it takes time, effort, and a little luck.

Given the competitive nature of the job, you should plan on getting an undergraduate degree. Also not required but highly recommended is an advanced degree in business, law, or marketing. A law degree is especially desirable because you'll be doing much of your work on clients' contracts.

Once you have the necessary educational components taken care of, it's time to get your foot on the first rung of the sports agents ladder. For many that means starting out at as an apprentice in a firm. This step gives you a chance to learn the nuts and bolts of the business. The work probably won't be all that exciting; some of it might be downright drudgery. But if you're motivated, hardworking, and willing to learn, this could be a valuable experience and set you up for a bright future.

Once you've completed your apprenticeship, there are several options available. You could go to work for a full-service,

AT A GLANCE

Salary Range

Each agency has a different method of compensation. Some get a percentage of an athlete's earnings; others are paid by an hourly rate or a flat rate. Additionally, each of the four major professional sports—baseball, football, basketball, and hockey—set agents' maximum fees through their respective players' associations. In the National Football League, for instance, an agent can charge 4 percent: 3 percent for contract negotiation and 1 percent for money management. An agent also can charge an NFL player 20 percent of any endorsement deal negotiated. In Major League Baseball, an agent can collect 5 percent of the contract value. Generally, a successful agent can expect to earn between $150 and $600 an hour, after subtracting dues owed to his or her agency.

Education/Experience

An undergraduate degree in business, economics, management, marketing, accounting, or, in a perfect world, all of the above, probably isn't enough. An MBA or law degree, while not required, is almost always a plus.

Personal Attributes

For starters, you'll need to be intelligent, insightful, trustworthy, honest, hard-working, and reliable. Remember you're going to be working for an athlete whose prime concern is to maximize his professional career into a lifetime of financial security. You'll have to be an excellent negotiator. It also helps to have a thick skin, because sports agents aren't always held in the highest esteem.

Requirements

There's no certification required, nor is there a governing body that regulates the way sports agents do business. You may have to register as a sports agent, depending upon the state in which you work.

Outlook

Because professional sports have become so lucrative and so much a part of our society, talented sports

(continues)

one-stop shopping agency, such as International Management Group (IMG), headquartered in Cleveland. IMG was founded in 1960 by the late Mark McCormack, who signed Arnold Palmer, the pro golf icon, as his first client. Over the years, IMG has become a worldwide company that represents athletes, performing artists, writers, fashion models, broadcasters, and leading corporations.

An agency such as IMG employs the best of the best sports agents. It provides its clients with everything they need—from contract negotiations to investments, insurance, tax advice, endorsements, and counseling. Huge firms also have full-time lawyers, accountants, financial planners, and sports psychologists on staff. Whatever a client needs, one of these mega-agencies can provide it. It's truly one-stop shopping.

But just like some students prefer small colleges, some athletes might feel more comfortable being represented by a smaller agency. A cooperative agency might be for them. Cooperative agencies have smaller staffs and don't always provide the myriad services that a large agency such as IMG would provide. Instead, those services, when needed, are handled by outside professionals.

The advantage of a cooperative agency is the closer relationships that can exist between agent and client, because of the smaller client base. Athletes who choose to be represented by a cooperative agency usually play a more active role in their financial and career decisions.

Another type of agent is the person who chooses to go it alone. The individual agent might be someone who isn't a big fan of the corporate environment, and has the experience, work ethic, and personality to run a business.

The individual agent could also be someone who has such an extensive and affluent client base that he or she is able to provide the same level of service as one of the giant firms. One of the most famous individual agents is Drew Rosenhaus, who represents some of the most famous players in the National Football League, including Terrell Owens of the Philadelphia Eagles and Edgerrin James of the Indianapolis Colts.

As important as your educational background is, your personality matters most when it comes to being successful as a sports agent. It's imperative that you be able to cultivate relationships and be an effective communicator. Not everyone you negotiate with is going to be your best buddy, but it's very important that they respect you. Your personality, your professionalism, your integrity, and your sense of ethics will go a long way toward your success and that of your clients.

Pitfalls

The job of a sports agent can involve considerable travel, long hours, and having to be at the beck and call of athletes who may think that they are your only focus. Be prepared to sacrifice personal time, maybe even family time, in service of your clients. Being a sports agent is definitely a 24-7 occupation.

Jay Burton, sports agent

Jay Burton never longed to be a sports agent when he grew up, because back then, in the 1960s and 70s, there were few careers as sports agents. "I didn't know what a sports agent was or what one did," says Burton. "I would argue that none of us did at the time. The colleges and universities did not offer extensive sports management curriculums like they do today."

When Burton was growing up, professional athletes pretty much accepted the contract the team offered them. The player's option was to either take it or leave it, which wasn't exactly an ideal situation if you were a player.

But things began to change in 1960, when Mark McCormick founded the International Management Group (IMG), a company that would represent athletes in contract negotiations and endorsement deals, and advise them on financial matters and retirement planning. IMG's first client was Arnold Palmer, one of the most famous golfers in history.

It wasn't long before IMG began representing athletes in professional team sports. Today, virtually every professional athlete is represented by a sports agent. It is a field that has grown markedly since its rather humble beginnings.

Burton became a sports agent by accident, not by design. He graduated from Heidelberg College in Tiffin, Ohio in 1976 with an associate degree in German and got a bachelor's degree in business the following year from Lake Erie College in Painesville, Ohio. His first job was what you'd expect: He joined the accounting firm of Arthur Young & Co. (since renamed Ernst & Young). He'd been there for seven years when a friend called.

"He wanted to know if I would be interested in possibly coming to work at IMG in their client financial department," Burton says. "I really didn't know too much about IMG, but after doing some homework on the company, I was intrigued."

What Burton discovered was that IMG was rapidly expanding and was in need of a financial planner in their golf division. "Three months and 14 interviews later, I made the decision to leave the 'conventional' business world and join this small—albeit growing—sports management firm," says Burton, who took a small cut in pay when he made the move. "I was immediately assigned to PGA [Professional Golf Association] and LPGA [Ladies Professional Golf Association] clients as their financial planner. It took a little time to get over the awe of it all, such as being in the locker room at the PGA Championship, but I soon came to realize that these were normal people who simply needed someone to take care of their financial matters."

But it didn't take long for Burton to connect with his clients on more than their money. He developed close relationships with many of them, becoming not just a financial planner, but their friend and loyal supporter as well. "I quickly learned that this was a 24-7 job in a personal services industry," Burton says.

It was that bond he forged with his clients that led Burton to becoming a full-time, full-fledged sports agent. When the agent representing IMG's LPGA players left the company, Burton was asked to replace him. In his new role, Burton wouldn't just manage the players' money, he'd be their overall manager, negotiating endorsement contracts and advising them on all aspects of their careers. "I thought it would be a gamble in some ways," he says, "but I also looked at it as an exciting opportunity."

(continues)

(continued)

It's an opportunity that he made the most of. More than 21 years later, Burton continues to enjoy his job as a sports agent, even though there's no such thing as a typical day. On any given day, Burton will deal with clients, talking to them about schedules, media obligations, and overseas opportunities; update sponsors on client performance; contact prospective sponsors; and recruit new clients. You can bet he has a cell phone plan with lots of free minutes.

All Burton's efforts are to ensure that his clients will get the most out of their careers, on the course and off. That can be a delicate balancing act, because too much off-the-course activity can keep a player from devoting the practice time necessary to maintain his or her level of play. But that's another important aspect of Burton's job: to guarantee that players don't over-schedule themselves.

"I truly enjoy adding value to a player's career," Burton says. "My goal is to allow them to focus on letting them become the best player they can be, leaving the rest of the off-course matters as my responsibility. Be it a small matter or an important achievement, such as delivering a significant multiyear endorsement contract, adding value to their life and career is what I like most about the job."

But every job has its downside, and being a sports agent is no different. Most of Burton's complaints center on time and travel. Sometimes there's not enough of one (time) and too much of another (travel). "Sometimes the travel can be a real pain," Burton says. "It may sound glamorous on the surface, but try racing from Gate H1 to E27 at Chicago's O'Hare on a late Friday afternoon, when you know if you don't make your connection, you won't get home to see your son's hockey game that evening.

"Too many times, travel interferes with the quality of your personal life. As much as I love my job, I also enjoy having a personal life, but sometimes the two can conflict. I try my best to keep it balanced, but as this is truly a 24-7 career, it's not always possible.

"Even with the demands of my IMG career, I appreciate the fact that most of my clients respect my personal time for the most part. One of my clients called me six days into my vacation this summer and asked, 'Aren't you glad I waited all week to bother you?' "

Burton says the field can be tough to break into, and once you've got your foot in the door, getting to the top doesn't happen overnight. "However, if you stay the course, get a little luck and good timing to come your way, and most of all put in a lot of hard work," he says, "it can lead to a rewarding financial career path."

Perks

While the travel may be a drawback for some people, others view it as a benefit. The opportunity to attend a variety of sporting events, some of which could be major happenings such as the Super Bowl or the World Series, is quite the perk for a lot of people. And then there's the money: If you reach the top of your profession, you will be extremely well compensated.

Get a Jump on the Job

One of the best ways to find out about the life of a sports agent is to secure an internship at a firm, where you will be exposed to the operations of each department. Internships are very difficult to come by, however. At IMG, for example, approximately 1,000 applications are received each year, with only 70 getting placed in one of the company's 21 North American offices.

SPORTSCASTER

OVERVIEW

If you're one of those people who loves sports, hates to miss a game on TV, and is sick for days when your favorite team loses, chances are you've thought about how absolutely, positively cool it would be to work as a sportscaster.

Imagine getting to broadcast every game, traveling with the team, getting to know the players, and even having the team for which you broadcast get all the way to a World Series or a Super Bowl.

As jobs go, they don't get much better than that. If you're determined enough and talented enough to make it as a broadcaster for a professional sports team or major college team, or for a network such as ABC, CBS, NBC, or ESPN, you will have indeed reached the pinnacle of your profession.

Network and major-market jobs are very tough to come by. The competition is fierce and the number of applicants far outnumbers the available jobs. You'll have to pay your dues before you make the leap to the big time, because this is one job in which you must work your way up the career ladder, starting at the entry level. You'll have to start with a healthy passion for sports. If you're not crazy about sports, if you're not anxious to hear and read and learn all that you can, you might be wise to consider another profession, because your lack of passion is likely to show through in your broadcasts.

Right up there with a passion for sports is the need to have a well-rounded knowledge about sports. Not just the names, the statistics, and the answers to every trivia question under the sun, but an

AT A GLANCE

Salary Range

It depends upon the size of the market, whether you're working on television or radio, and the level of sports you're broadcasting (high school, college, minor league, or professional sports). The top broadcasters that you hear regularly on television—Jim Nantz, Joe Buck, Al Michaels, and Brent Musburger, to name a few—make huge salaries, easily more than $1 million a year. But the individual men and women working at the local radio station, calling high school football and basketball games, may be lucky to pull in $20,000 a year.

Education/Experience

Many high schools have their own television stations, which provide an excellent opportunity to get your feet wet and learn the basics of broadcasting. Any broadcasting experience is helpful. As far as education is concerned, a communications degree should serve you well. You'll also need solid writing skills, so make sure you take courses to help develop that talent. One of the most important factors is getting experience while you're getting a college degree, whether through an internship or part-time job at a radio or TV station.

Personal Attributes

For starters, a controlled, well-modulated, and pleasant speaking voice helps. You'll also need to be enthusiastic, able to ad-lib, and a quick study. An easygoing personality also helps because it's important that your listeners like you. And let's not forget about your knowledge of sports. You should be the type of person that can't enough of sports, whether it's from television, radio, newspapers, magazines, or books.

Requirements

You don't need a college degree, and you don't need to be a member of any organization to become a successful play-by-play announcer, although both might come in handy. Joining the

(continues)

appreciation for the strategy of the games and the nuances that make each sport a drama unto itself.

If you've got the basics taken care of, the next step is getting as much experience as you can as early as you can. If you're in high school or college, try to work for the student television and/or radio station. And when you're not broadcasting, you should try to practice whenever you can. Turn on a game, turn down the sound, and do your own play-by-play by talking into a tape recorder. Any practice is beneficial practice.

When it comes to choosing a major in college, you won't go wrong with a degree in communications. But again, it's the experience that counts. More than likely, you'll have to start at the local level after you graduate, working for TV and radio stations in small markets and broadcasting high school or college games. No, it's not glamorous, but in many cases it's necessary. The next step up might be a job working for a minor league team in baseball, hockey, or basketball.

But regardless of the size of the market or the stature of the team you're broadcasting, you'll have to do several things to be successful: inform, entertain, and educate. The best announcers not only tell their listeners or viewers what happened, but why it happened, and they're able to do it in such a way that satisfies the diehard fan and doesn't overwhelm the casual fan. They also will have done enough homework to throw in an anecdote here and there to help keep the audience interested. Part of that homework involves asking the right questions to players and coaches in order to get pertinent information.

Perhaps a play-by-play announcer's most important attribute is credibility. Especially if you're doing radio broadcasts, your audience has to trust you to give them a balanced view of what's taking place on the field. There's no place in the broadcast booth for "homers" who spin everything in favor of their team. You also can improve your style by listening to established broadcasters—people who have been in the business for a while and have done a variety of sports. You don't want to copy their style or use any of their trademark lines, but it wouldn't hurt to pick up a few tips, to learn the do's and don'ts, and to know when to speak and when to be quiet. Sometimes a broadcaster's silence can be every bit as eloquent as anything he or she would say.

Pitfalls

The travel can be brutal, especially if you broadcast baseball, basketball, or hockey, all of which play a lot of road games. If you happen to broadcast these sports at the minor league level, then the travel problem is compounded because much of the travel is done by bus. As for the pay scale, you won't get rich, unless you make it to a

Steve Degler, sportscaster

Like most kids growing up, Steve Degler was a sports fanatic. No matter what sport was in season, there was always a game going on involving the kids in his neighborhood. Baseball, football, or basketball, you name it, Degler and his friends played it as often and as long as they could.

But before he reached adolescence, he came to a very important realization. "I knew by about the age of 12 that I would never be good enough to be a professional athlete," Degler says.

So he went to plan B.

"I decided that the next best thing to being an athlete would be broadcasting the games," he says. "So I would 'broadcast' along with the TV announcers, while I watched a game, or I would do the play-by-play for a baseball board game—yes, a board game—that I always played."

Degler was a boy with a dream. Eventually, his childhood hobby turned into a career. He graduated from Kutztown University in southeastern Pennsylvania in 1988 with a bachelor's degree in telecommunications. Soon afterward, he entered the business on the ground floor. He started doing play-by-play and color commentary for local radio stations that broadcast high school football and basketball games. From 1989 through 1991, he also did some part-time radio and TV broadcasting for the Reading Phillies, a Class-AA minor league affiliate of the Philadelphia Phillies. Then, in 1992, the Reading Phillies were looking for a full-time radio announcer, and Degler got the call. The 2005 season was his 15th with the ballclub.

Degler usually arrives at the stadium about three hours before the game starts, which tells you that there's more to his job than sitting behind a microphone and telling fans what's happening. "Getting there early gives me time to go through statistics, set up equipment, and do any interviews that might be necessary for the pregame show," Degler says. "I may need to talk to coaches to get specific information on players or to find out what they need to do in order to win the game.

"There is quite a bit of time spent preparing for the broadcast. I feel the easy part is doing the game. Once the action starts, it's time to relax and have fun."

And fun is what Degler has each time he calls a game.

"Broadcasting doesn't feel like a job, and every day is different," he says. "I get paid to talk about games, and that's a lot of fun. I enjoy high school, college, and professional games. I try to prepare the same for all three levels.

"With broadcasting you never know what you might see. A pitcher might throw a no-hitter, a running back may score five touchdowns, or a basketball player could score 40 points. It is definitely not a profession where you do or see the same things every day."

Once the Reading Phillies season is over, Degler broadcasts a variety of different sports, including Albright College football, La Salle University basketball, and high school and college football and basketball games throughout the mid-Atlantic region.

Degler's varied schedule means two things: One, he has to be familiar with many different sports, coaches, and players. To gain that familiarity, he has to spend a lot of time doing his homework—learning names and uniform numbers, getting to know the people he'll be covering, understanding how the team he's covering relates to the rest of the league it's in. As you can see, he isn't blessed with a lot of spare time.

The second thing Degler's hectic schedule guarantees is a lot of travel, which, not surprisingly, happens to be the downside of his job.

(continues)

(continued)

"I will broadcast more than 200 games in a year and travel close to 20,000 miles annually," says Degler, who is married with two young daughters. "And not every game is close to home. I probably spend about 75 days a year—maybe more—in a hotel room. Being away from my family is without a doubt the toughest part of being a sportscaster."

If Degler had a job as the play-by-play man for a professional team, one in Major League Baseball or the National Football League, his travel would be on airplanes. Unfortunately, minor league baseball teams go from city to city on buses. Most of the rest of his commutes once baseball season is over are made by car.

Degler says the key to becoming a successful play-by-play announcer is paying your dues. "You usually don't begin your career at ESPN or NBC," he says. "You have to work your way up through the ranks." He thinks the best way to begin that process of working your way up the ranks is to adopt the slogan used by the Boy Scouts: Be prepared. "Always have more material to use on the air than you need," Degler says. "You can't run out of things to say in a broadcast."

He offers a few other tips to help you along the way: Know the rules of the game, so if something unusual happens, you'll be able to explain the situation. Know how to ask relevant questions so that you get answers and information that you can use later. Never turn down an opportunity to get experience. If you have a chance to do a live event on the air—even if you're not crazy about the event—do it. By doing the little things, employers will keep you in mind when it comes to doing bigger events.

"One of the most important things is to have fun," Degler says. "It's a game and you're getting paid to be there. What could be better?"

large market and broadcast for professional sports teams or big-time college programs.

Perks

If you love sports, this job is the equivalent of heaven. You not only get a great seat at the game, but you become one of the fans' primary links to their favorite teams. In many cases, the broadcaster for a team can become as popular as the players.

Get a Jump on the Job

Get as much experience as possible. This is one job in which there is no such thing as too much experience. And in addition to working for your high school or college television station or a local radio station, you can also work on your delivery by talking into a tape recorder while you're watching a game.

SPORTS INFORMATION DIRECTOR

OVERVIEW

If you like sports, and you like being around athletes and coaches, sports information director could be the perfect job for you.

To become a successful sports information director, you'll need a variety of skills, because the job entails many duties and responsibilities. In general terms, a sports information director has to serve as the institution's representative to the media for all the athletic programs, plan and schedule all activities involving the media, write and distribute news releases to all media, and compile media guides.

That list might not seem too overwhelming, but those duties have to be performed for every sport at the school. If you were the sports information director at a major university, such as Penn State, you'd have 29 intercollegiate sports to handle. Of course, you'd have assistant sports information directors and a group of student interns, as well, but handling media activities and publications for 29 sports is a full-time job, and then some.

Not every sport requires the same amount of time. The football program at Penn State would command considerably more attention and manpower than the fencing team. (Yes, there is an intercollegiate fencing team at Penn State.) But still, there's a lot of work involved. One other thing to remember is that football isn't the only sport that's played in the fall. There's

AT A GLANCE

Salary Range

What you earn depends on the size of the college or university. Entry-level jobs pay approximately $30,000 a year. Should you be hired by a major university with high-profile teams, you could earn as much as $125,000 to $130,000 annually.

Education/Experience

A bachelor's degree is required. Sports information directors may have degrees in a variety of disciplines—such as math, science, political science, or journalism. What counts as much as or more than the degree is the practical experience you've gained along the way. More and more applicants for sports information director jobs have master's degrees, because the field has become so competitive.

Personal Attributes

You will be dealing with a variety of people—players and coaches at your school, the media, professors and staff from your school, counterparts from other schools ... and the list goes on. You'll need a pleasant, upbeat, and energetic personality. You'll also be doing a lot of scheduling and record-keeping, so it helps to be organized and detail-oriented.

Requirements

There is no standard you have to meet to become a sports information director, nor is there a test you have to pass. While it's not required, becoming a member of the College Sports Information Directors of America would be beneficial, because of the contacts you'll make and the support you'll receive, in terms of workshops and publications.

Outlook

The job market for sports information directors has become more and more competitive, with many jobs requiring a master's degree. Be prepared to work hard, be patient, and knock on a lot of doors.

also men's soccer, field hockey, women's volleyball, cross country, and golf.

So let's take a look at what a sports information director might do during a week of the football season, which is the most important season at many schools.

Each reporter covering the game needs a credential that guarantees access to the press box and locker rooms. It's up to the sports information director to approve those reporters requesting credentials and to make sure there is a seat for them in the press box. It's not unusual to have as many as 200 reporters to cover regular season games at major universities.

Photographers and cameramen also need credentials, which ensure them access to the sidelines during the game and the locker rooms after the game.

Prior to each game, a press release is prepared with a look back at the previous game and a preview of the next game. The release includes statistics, rosters, and lineups for both teams; quotes from players and coaches; and interesting notes and tidbits that will add to the media's coverage.

The release is usually sent electronically to the media early in the week so it can be used for reference by reporters for their preview stories.

Reporters also want to talk to the players and coaches during the week. Most coaches have teleconferences early in the week, but player interviews with individual reporters are arranged by the sports information director. The more high profile the school and its football program, the more reporters there are to satisfy.

If a game is to be televised, the sports information director helps the television production crew get ready for the game, arranging pregame interviews with the head coach and selected players and providing much of the information you hear during the telecast.

On game day, the sports information director and his or her support personnel are responsible for keeping statistics and making sure the media are kept up to date on things such as records set, streaks that are extended or ended, and updates on player injuries.

When the game is over, there are post-game interviews to arrange with coaches and players and a complete packet of game stats to produce. Before you know it, the entire process starts over again for the next game.

Football is just one of several sports that get a similar treatment.

One element of that treatment is the media guide produced for most sports by the sports information director's office. Issued prior to the start of each sport's season, they include profiles of players and coaches, detailed statistics from the previous season, a capsule look at opponents, a historical record book of the program, and interesting facts about the program and the school.

As you can see, the job of a sports information director is labor-intensive and requires expert organizational skills. But if you like sports and you're willing to work hard, it could be just the ticket for you.

Pitfalls

The schedule can be hectic and the hours can be long. You also can expect to work plenty of nights and most weekends. There is also a fair amount of travel involved, because the sports information director often accompanies teams to road games.

Perks

You're around coaches and athletes, and an essential part of your job is to attend games,

Mike Enright, sports information director

There are no major professional sports teams in Connecticut—no baseball, football, basketball, or hockey. As a result, the state's newspapers and television and radio stations focus the majority of their attention primarily on two teams: the University of Connecticut men's and women's basketball teams.

Both teams have been among the very best in the United States over the past 10 to 15 years. The media contingent that covers them is one of the largest in the country.

The men's team is covered on a regular basis by nine daily newspapers, four television stations, and a 50,000-watt radio station that can be heard as far west as Ohio and as far south as the Carolinas. It's not unusual for as many as 200 media members to request press credentials for a regular season men's basketball game.

Mike Enright, the associate athletic director/communications, is in charge of the University of Connecticut communications staff. It's his job to ensure that the "horde," as it's called, gets the necessary information and access.

"Because there are no pro teams, we get a large chunk of the coverage," Enright says. "That can be a good thing and a bad thing sometimes. We certainly get a huge chunk of attention, but every time you have a little blemish, it becomes a major story in the state. Other schools with pro teams in their coverage area, if they have a little blemish, it often gets lost in the shuffle."

Enright, a native of Connecticut, graduated from the University of Connecticut in 1988. While he was in school, he worked in the sports information director's office as a student assistant. He wrote basic press releases and prepared statistics for the media.

Eventually, he got to attend and work at games, and during the summers, he worked in the sports department of the *Norwich* (Conn.) *Bulletin*.

"I value that experience [with the newspaper] to this day," Enright says. "It gave me a chance to see the other side of the public relations business. It also gave me a chance to get involved in communications, understanding the media, writing. You don't need to major in communications to be in communications. You just have to get involved."

Enright graduated from the University of Connecticut in 1988 and joined the sports information department soon afterward. He stayed until 1992, when he took a job at the University of Notre Dame, where one of his main responsibilities was the football program. If you know anything about college sports, you know that the Notre Dame football team is one of the most popular in the country.

In 2000 and 2001, Enright was among those in the Notre Dame sports information office to win awards, presented by the College Sports Information Directors Association of America, for the annual football guides. Enright left Notre Dame after two years to take the top job at Boston College. Two years later, in 2002, he returned to Connecticut, where he was named an associate athletic director.

For Enright, a typical day—if there is such a thing in his business—begins at home, where he scans local and national newspapers to see what "people are writing about us.

"By the time I get my dog to the bottom of the driveway and see the *Hartford Courant*," he says, "I have a pretty good idea of what kind of a day I'm going to have."

(continues)

(continued)

One aspect of his business that has changed dramatically, says Enright, is the way information is communicated. It used to be that you got much of your sports news from newspapers and a five-minute segment on the 6 p.m. and 11 p.m. newscasts. No more.

"Over the last 10 or 15 years, the Internet has changed everything," Enright says. "There's been a media explosion; information travels so much more quickly. Because of that, you have to think ahead, more than you had to before, which is more of a challenge."When he arrives at his office, he takes care of some paperwork and makes sure the assistants and interns, many of whom handle the non-major sports, are in good shape. He usually meets with the athletic director once a day, and then during the afternoon will attend practices to make sure the media have what they need.

"The amount of time the job takes does not allow for a lot of free time," says Enright, who is married and has a young son. "A lot of times this job can be 24-7; you feel as if you're on call if you're not working. I always have my cell phone ready, day or night.

"You have to love it for all the time and effort you have to put into it."

And what Enright loves most about it are the people.

"That's the best part, the people you work with," he says. "The coaches, players … I have a lot of friends in the media. Everyone I deal with has a lot of passion for what they do. I get to work with some pretty interesting people.

"The job has got its glamorous moments, but it also has a lot of unglamorous moments. It's got its highs, you bet, and it's got its tedious moments. But every job, no matter what it is has its tedious moments."

If you're considering a career in sports information, Enright suggests being the manager of a high school team, writing for the school paper, or for the student television station. "You want to learn all you can about all aspects of sports," he says. "But if you decide to enter this field, it's important that you know what you're getting yourself into. There are a lot of great moments, but it takes a lot of hard work. There are a lot of hours, a lot of weekends, a lot of nights. Your social life might take a little bit of a hit. There can be a lot of travel. Sometimes it's glamorous, sometimes it's not. But I know I love being able to work with kids to promote all the good things they do."

---

which, if you're a sports fan, can be as good as it gets. Plus, you might get to travel to interesting places and major sporting events.

Get a Jump on the Job

You can gain valuable experience by writing for your high school and college newspapers or working for your school's television or radio station. Maybe you could keep statistics for an athletic team or land an internship in the sports information office.

SPORTS MASCOT

OVERVIEW

Being a sports mascot involves more than just jumping around during the game and inciting the crowd to whoop and holler. You're also expected to make personal appearances—lots of them—at local shopping malls, meeting and greeting fans. You may appear at local schools or in parades. As a professional team mascot, you're the face of the team and a real draw—especially for kids.

Ever since the 1800s, we've had the idea that a mascot brings good luck—and today, the professional sports mascot represents a community's team all year long. The mascot's face is everywhere—on press releases, posters, tickets, ads, on team T-shirts, jerseys, jackets, bumper stickers, and pennants. Everybody knows their team mascot, which makes that furry funny face a vital marketing tool for the team. The mascot serves as a team's walking billboard.

This high-profile position is a real career, and one within your reach—if you're the right kind of person. Team mascots dress up in costumes representing their team, entertain the crowd, and act as comic cheerleaders. When an opening occurs, the team will hold auditions, looking to hire someone based on the energy of the person's performance rather than educational qualifications.

Typically, the team mascot will be everywhere during the game—the crowds can spot him leaping, dancing, running, jumping, skating, or sliding with various props. One minute he's in the stands,

AT A GLANCE

Salary Range
A low of $20 per game to an annual high salary of six figures.

Education/Experience
You can't major in professional team mascot, but experience does count here. You need to work your way up the ladder. If you're still in high school, begin there, move on to college mascot work, and then get into minor league teams. Eventually you can make it to the big leagues.

Personal Attributes
You've got to be outgoing, great with a crowd, a bit of a stuntperson, and good at miming. Loving kids is a plus, since you'll be going to lots of schools and interacting with kids at the games.

Requirements
You've got to be energetic, in excellent physical shape, savvy enough to be able to read a crowd, and able to withstand extremely hot temperatures for long periods of time. You've also got to be clever enough to come up with solid routines and be physically able to fall on your face, tumble down the stairs, and so on.

Outlook
Fair. While there are lots of minor and major sports teams, all of whom have mascots, there are typically only one or two mascots per team.

hugging a little kid or mugging for photos, the next he's down on the field roughing up the ump. Kids trail behind him, clamoring for his autograph or just a quick hug. He's always *on*, energetic, getting the crowd aroused and laughing. He may be called upon to come up with skits or follow a script, or simply improvise funny stuff to make the crowd laugh. Yet there are strict rules for this

Dean Stump, sports mascot

From September to June, you can find Dean Stump teaching elementary health and phys ed in Antietam School District in Pennsylvania. But once school is out for the summer, Stump leaves behind the world of chalk dust and gymnasiums for the baseball stadium in Reading, Pennsylvania.

Ever since 1998, Stump has been the fellow buried under the giant baseball head—he's Screwball, the primary mascot for the Reading Phillies, the farm team for the Philadelphia Phillies baseball club.

As Screwball, Stump appears at most of the 71 home games and also makes numerous personal appearances, although he doesn't do all the personal appearances (he has apprentices who help out). He also plays the drums with the Mascot Band, including the other Reading Philly mascots: Change-Up the turtle, Bucky the beaver, Blooper the dog, and Quack the duck.

"I like being able to act on a whim, and not feel any kind of embarrasment," he says. "No one knows it's you in there." Standing 6 foot 6 inches in the costume, he's clothed in a red and white outfit decorated with red fur.

Still, it's not a job for the faint of heart—it can get mighty hot inside that giant baseball head. "Temperatures can get up to between 130 and 140 degrees [F]," Stump says. "I used to wear ice, but it got cumbersome, and I was getting a lot of sinus problems and colds. So I stopped using ice." It's not so bad, he says—"at least I've never passed out!"

Stump is given basic scripts by the front office, and must be able to hit his marks and be at the right spot to lead cheers and hand out pizzas to the crowd. He practices his walk and gestures, and is proud of the fact that in spite of the towering head he wears, he can still do a cartwheel in costume. "You gotta keep the crowds entertained," he explains. "You've got to keep them thinking!" About 60 percent of the people who come up to him are kids. Because the club wants its mascots to be accessible, anyone in the stands can meet any of the mascots. "It can be difficult," Stump says, "because some kids want more attention than others."

comedian-in-a-suit. As a mascot, you must know your role and play it to the hilt, while keeping it clean and wholesome. You've got to be able to entertain both kids and adults at the same time and never, ever break character.

If you're drawn to this kind of wacky world, you'll need to start by contacting local sports teams. At a small operation, you should talk to someone in promotions; bigger teams will steer you to someone in public affairs, public relations, or community development. You don't have to start off with the big chicken feet,

either; maybe you can start helping out at games during various promotional activities. You might help toss T-shirts into the stands, lug free pizzas around to donate to some lucky fan, or splash water on the performers.

Pitfalls

Let's face it, it's hot and stinky in those mascot costumes, and it can be physically draining work. Mascots typically sweat about 10 pounds off each game, staggering under that load of fur and feathers in 100-plus degree heat. In fact,

Although Screwball gives autographs, it's hard to do out on the field. "It's much easier in the autograph booth," he explains.

Stump loves his work, but there can be problems in dealing with smart-aleck teenagers. Even worse are the rude people and inebriated fans, who can be "a problem," he says, "but you learn to tolerate it." In any case, he tries to stay away from sections that serve beer during the game.

Because his vision is limited inside the giant baseball head, Stump always has one or two "handlers" with him as he plows along through the stands. "They can alert you to what's around you," he explains. "It's hard to see below you, and it's hard to see the little kids who come up and want to hug your ankles."

If you're interested in working as a sports mascot, Stump advises you to start small—try out for your local high school mascot. "If your school doesn't have a mascot, then watch other schools' mascots," he says. "Watch what others are doing, and watch mascots of national teams, such as the Philly Phanatic or the San Diego Chicken." Stump himself did a lot of acting in high school.

The Reading Phillies are enormously popular summer entertainment in the Reading area, famous for attracting hordes of families on summer nights who come out for safe, clean fun and for the very inexpensive seats, food, and entertainment. There are always lots of contests, free giveaways, and audience participation. The best part of the job, Stump says, is that he's there to "make people feel like they're an important part of the game."

He so enjoys his work that he's brought his son into the stadium, as a bat boy. "It's become a family thing," he says. "I'd like to do it until my daughter's ready to take over. I look at it as a great hobby, as a good outlet. I'll do this as long as I want to do it and as long as they'll let me!"

in one study, 43 percent of sports mascots suffer heat-related illnesses. Injuries aren't unheard of, either—ankle sprains are the most common, because it's not easy traipsing around in a costume that typically features really big floppy shoes or stuffed feet. Mascots also face the risk of being physically attacked by the opposing team's fans.

Perks

You get paid to watch games and make people laugh—can it get any better than that?

Get a Jump on the Job

If you've got a hankering to dress up in a funny costume and run around a sports stadium, you can start with your high school mascot. Don't worry about working for free—that's the best way to get experience. Try on the costume and work at a couple of games to see if it seems like something you'd like to do. You can continue your efforts at the collegiate level if you wish, which will put you in a good position for landing a mascot gig for a professional team someday.

SPORTS PHOTOGRAPHER

OVERVIEW

Sports photographers use cameras to record action that occurs during games and other sporting events. They cover all types of sports, from high school to professional, and their work situations vary greatly.

Some sports photographers work on their own as freelancers. That means they have to keep hustling to make sure they have enough work. Other sports photographers work for newspapers, where they may shoot only sports, but most likely will have other types of assignments, as well. Magazines also hire sports photographers, as do agencies and companies that distribute sports photos to media all around the world. Sports photographers work for companies that manufacture sports cards, Web sites, and wire services. Some sports photographers pick up extra income on youth league picture days, when each kid has his or her picture taken in uniform and different packages are offered to parents.

Probably all of these work scenarios have their advantages and disadvantages. Photographers who work for newspapers and magazines (except for major publications) don't earn all that much money, but at least you can count on a paycheck. Top-rate freelance photographers who are in demand can make very good money, but there's a lot of scrambling involved to getting to that level. You have to be willing to travel, put in long hours, and work nights and weekends, when many—probably most—sports events occur. And, freelance

AT A GLANCE

Salary Range

The salary of a sports photographer varies greatly, depending on the type and location of employment, how well the photographer is known, experience, and other factors. The average yearly salary for a full-time sports photographer ranges from about $35,000 to $50,000.

Education/Experience

There are no set educational requirements for sports photographers. Plenty of photographers are self-trained, but getting a college degree in photojournalism or a related program will give you an advantage when you start hunting for work. Many schools, including technical schools, offer general photography courses, which also would be useful.

Personal Attributes

You'll need to be determined and have a lot of perseverance. Sports photography is a competitive field, and it can take some time to break into it. You should be knowledgeable about sports, and have a love for them, since you'll be spending a lot of time around them. And, of course, you also need to be knowledgeable about photography and photography equipment. You should be creative and detail oriented, and be able to make quick decisions about what and when to shoot. You also must have good communication skills and some writing skills to compose captions.

Requirements

You'll need credentials in order to cover games and sporting events. You can't just walk onto the golf course or into the end zone and starting taking pictures. Other requirements will vary, depending on your employer and other factors.

Outlook

Employment for sports photographers is expected to increase by about 10 percent through 2012, a growth rate that is considered average.

photographers also have to keep track of the business end of things, making sure to send out bills, pay bills, keep track of income for tax purposes, work to attract new clients through advertising or marketing, and so forth.

Sports photography is all about timing, and it takes a lot of practice to get that timing down to a science. A great catch—the moment a ball is snagged from air—lasts for only a fraction of a second. That doesn't give you a lot of time to plan and execute your shot. Taking pictures becomes almost instinctual to a great photographer, but it takes an awful lot of practice before that occurs.

Brad Wilder, freelance sports photographer

Brad Wilder is using his skills as a sports photographer to help pay his way through graduate school at the University of Kentucky in Lexington. Working through a New York City-based agency, Wilder is hired to photograph all of the university's football and basketball games. He also shoots baseball, soccer, and Nascar for various clients.

His work has been published in *ESPN the Magazine, US Weekly, Country Weekly,* and *Racing Fan Magazine,* and has appeared online at ESPN.com and CollegeSports.com. Not bad for a guy who only started in sports photography when he joined the yearbook staff as an undergraduate at the University of Kentucky.

"The yearbook needed a photographer to go and take pictures at the football games, so I said I would do it," Wilder said. "I didn't know too much about what I was doing, and my work reflected that. It really wasn't very good."

That opportunity, however, opened Wilder's eyes to the challenges and rewards of sports photography.

"I realized how much fun it was to photograph sports events, and I worked really, really hard to improve at it," Wilder said. "I studied and practiced, and practiced some more."

As his work improved, people began to take notice, and soon Wilder was offering his services as a freelance photographer to area newspapers, magazines, Web sites, and wire services.

"I've been lucky, but I've worked very hard, too," he said. "I feel like I put in my time and paid my dues at first, and now it's starting to pay off for me. It took me a few years to get to this point, and that's faster than it happens for a lot of people."

Wilder advised anyone interested in becoming a sports photographer to not only learn everything you can about photography, but get as familiar as you can with the basics of every sport. After all, he said, you can't know what to shoot if you don't know what is important to a particular sport. It's also important to work on improving your reaction times and reflexes, he said. You'll only have a second to make a shot, and, if you hesitate, that second will be lost.

And, he said, start saving your money now so you'll be able to buy the equipment you'll need.

"I've really kept my equipment to a minimum while I'm still in school, and I've bought it all used," Wilder said. "Still, I have more than $5,000 worth and there's still a lot more I need to get."

The best part of the job, Wilder said, is watching his work get better and better.

"That's the best thing for me," he said. "I look back on the photos I did when I was first starting out with the yearbook staff, and I can't believe how bad they look. It's nice to look at my work now and see how much it's improved."

The bottom line is, if you're a good photographer, and you can deliver what you promise, you'll do all right for yourself.

Pitfalls

Sports photography jobs don't grow on trees, and there tends to be a fair amount of competition for them. If you're a freelance photographer, or even if you're employed and want to do some extra work on the side, as many photographers do, you're going to need some expensive equipment. It can cost up to $35,000 to get all the equipment necessary to professional photography. Most sports photographers find their jobs to be really exciting and challenging, at first. Over time, however, the job can become a bit tedious.

Perks

If you like sports, you're in luck, because you'll be watching a lot of them. Top-rate sports photographers get to go to all the big sporting events, from the Super Bowl to the World Series to the Olympic Games. And rubbing elbows with the players is part of the deal. Full-time sports photographers do a lot of traveling, so you'll get to see some places you might not otherwise visit.

Get a Jump on the Job

Look at all the sports photos that you can find. Check out *Sports Illustrated* and *ESPN The Magazine* at every chance, and look carefully at how the photos are taken. Check out sports photography books in your local bookstore or library and study the photos they contain. Spend some time on SportsShooter.com, a great resource for sports photographers and those who aspire to be (the Web site is described in Appendix A). Once you've gotten an idea of what good sports photos look like, grab whatever equipment you have and start practicing. Start by taking pictures at Little League games, kids' soccer games, or even kids shooting hoops at the local playground. These types of events are great because you can get close to the action. You'll need credentials to photograph high school games, so the alternative is to shoot from the stands using a telephoto lens. Once your photos start to look the way you want them to, begin building up a portfolio. Once you feel like your shots are on par with what you see published locally, contact your local newspaper and see if they're looking for any extra help with photography. Keep practicing and experiment with different lights, camera angles, and so forth. Take photography classes at a local arts institute, vocational center, or community college.

SPORTS PSYCHOLOGIST

OVERVIEW

It used to be that when a professional athlete talked about getting better, it meant getting better in the physical sense—practicing longer, lifting more weights, doing more running, saying no to that extra slice of pizza. But things have changed over the years. These days, athletes don't just concentrate on improving their size, strength, speed and stamina—they're also concerned about being in the best mental shape possible.

Enter the sports psychologist. Many top-flight athletes consider their sports psychologist to be as important as their personal fitness trainer, their nutritionist, or their agent.

Often times, the difference between success and failure is a matter of mind. For instance, any golfer who qualifies to play on the PGA Tour, which features the best players in the world, has the physical tools necessary for success. Tour players are able to hit it a long way, get out of trouble when they hit it off line, save strokes around the greens, and make putts when they have to. If they couldn't do those things, they wouldn't have made it to the PGA Tour in the first place.

But the difference between being a great player and a good player, between flourishing or foundering under pressure, can be a person's ability to handle stress.

Can you imagine how nervous you'd be if you had to sink a putt worth $1 million? It would be difficult for most people to keep their knees from knocking together, let alone be able to take the putter back and through the ball.

By working with a sports psychologist, the golfer, in this case, would have been taught tips and tricks to help control his emotions and to keep him in the proper frame of mind, no matter how stressful the situation. Perhaps he learned how to remain focused on the present or he visualized a positive outcome before he stepped up to hit the putt.

Having the right mindset can be every bit as important as having the right putting technique.

Dr. Deborah Graham, sports psychologist

Growing up in Sabinal, Texas, a small town about 60 miles west of San Antonio, Deborah Graham loved sports. She was an athlete who wanted to get a job in a sports-related field. So she attended Baylor University, graduated in 1976 with a bachelor's degree in physical education and business, and then discovered that jobs weren't all that plentiful. "Outside of teaching tennis privately, I found it difficult to get a job in education, because of declining enrollments," Graham says. "And I saw no other venues to work with athletes without an advanced degree."

So instead of drawing a paycheck as a phys ed teacher, Graham became a student again, this time heading to California. In 1980, she received a master's degree in psychology from Azusa Pacific University, and in the same year she received a tempting opportunity: The state of California offered to continue her tuition scholarship, paying for her doctoral studies, if she continued her education. "I found that hard to decline," she says.

Graham earned her doctorate in counseling psychology in 1982 from the United States International University in San Diego, where she completed an internship under Dr. Richard Lister, a noted sports psychologist and former athlete. That internship proved to be the start of something big.

Lister encouraged Graham to do her dissertation on professional athletes. She chose women golfers, members of the Ladies Professional Golf Association Tour, because there was little research on them at the time. Graham's study compared personality scores of champion LPGA golfers against the scores of other LPGA golfers. She determined that champion golfers shared eight traits. They have an above-average ability to focus, are above-average in abstract thinking, are more emotionally stable, have above-average dominance, are more tough-minded, have above-average self-confidence, are more self-sufficient, and play with below-average levels of tension.

Graham didn't know it at the time, but determining those eight traits would be the foundation on which she would build her career. But before she found her niche, she spent about eight years in private practice. During that time, she repeated her golf study, using professional race car drivers, and also worked with some Olympic athletes.

When her husband suggested that she duplicate her LPGA study by using players on the PGA Tour and the Senior PGA Tour, Graham became a full-time sports psychologist.

Graham conducted the same personality inventory on the PGA and Senior PGA players.

"By the time I completed the study," Graham says, "I found that many of the players were eager to learn more, and asked to become clients. Soon I was extremely busy and had to choose between my full-time psychology practice in Southern California, which was partially sports oriented, and a full-time practice with professional golfers, which was mostly sports oriented. The choice was very easy. My dream had come true."

In 1989, Graham and Jon Stabler cofounded Golfpsych, a mental game system based on the research she did with the golf pros. She works with more than 300 clients on all the major golf tours.

For Graham, there is no such thing as a typical day, because every day brings something different. Most of her work is done from the Golfpsych headquarters in Boerne, Texas, where she can see clients in person or talk to them by phone.

"Some [clients] come for their first visit, some come intermittently, and some I have never met [personally]," Graham says. "In a single day I might be on the phone, in the office, or at the golf course—sometimes all three."

Because Graham is licensed to do personal counseling—many sports psychologists are not— she can also handle issues other than those dealing with performance enhancement.

"That really makes it fun for me," she says. "In a single day I might help clients with stress management, pain control, depression, organizational skills, bereavement, marriage counseling, divorce mediation. And at the same time, I can address the typical sports psychology issues related to focus, concentration, thought control, confidence, tough-mindedness, fear of failure, or fear of success. Basically, I deal with problem solving of all sorts."

In addition to her work with golf professionals and at Golfpsych, Graham also published *The Eight Traits of Champion Golfers,* in 1999, based on her doctoral dissertation.

Being a successful sports psychologist requires a "passion for sports, but even more a passion for helping others," according to Graham.

"I love to help clients maximize their potential in their sport, but the sport is really only a vehicle," she says. "For me, the real joy is helping people be their best in all aspects of their lives."

For students wishing to become sports psychologists, Graham says the first step is deciding what type you'd like to be: a researcher for a college or university; a lecturer, teacher, or professor with counseling responsibilities for a college or university; a counseling sports psychologist for a team; or a self-employed, licensed counseling and sports psychologist.

"My recommendations are related to the final choice," Graham says. "If this is your choice, be certain that you have a passion for sport, but even more a passion for helping others. Relatively few seem to find their niche doing this wonderful profession full time on their own, so be relentless and determined. Your life will be enriched by the many grateful souls you will be blessed to be able to help, all using the wonderful medium of sports."

And while sports psychologists are most often thought of as working with individual athletes, such as golfers and tennis players, most professional teams and many major college programs have someone on staff to deal with the mental well being of their athletes.

Sports psychologists aren't limited to working with elite athletes, either. Because of the explosion of youth sports and the lure of college scholarships and pro careers, parents are taking their children to see sports psychologists in order to give them every advantage possible.

There are also opportunities in this field that don't necessarily involve dealing one-on-one with athletes. You could do research, lecture or teach about sports psychology at a college or university.

Pitfalls

Depending on what educational path you choose, the academic demands could be rigorous. There also could be considerable travel involved and long hours.

Perks

Helping athletes deal with their problems and ultimately realize their full potential is the best reward. And if you're a sports fan, which you should be to work in this field, being around highly motivated athletes would be a real plus.

Get a Jump on the Job

It would help to learn as much as you can about sports so that you can appreciate the problems and pressures athletes must deal with. Taking psychology courses in high school would also be beneficial and give you a sneak peek at what lies ahead.

SPORTSWRITER, NEWSPAPER

OVERVIEW

As jobs go, being a sportswriter ranks pretty high on the cool scale. It's exciting, challenging, and rarely the same from one day to the next. It allows you to be creative and to be around sports. You get paid to watch games, interview athletes and coaches, and then tell your readers all about it.

Like any job, you have to pay your dues. The first step up the sportswriter ladder is likely to involve a certain amount of grunt work. No, it's not glamorous, but it's a good way to learn the nuts and bolts of the business.

You might be asked to answer phones, go through faxes and e-mails, and then take that information and write it for the paper. And yes, you might also be asked to get coffee or make a food run.

Granted, it's not quite as exciting as covering the big game or interviewing the star player, but keep in mind that someone is going to read it. That's why it's important to be careful when taking the information and to make absolutely sure the names are spelled correctly.

The next step up the ladder is getting a high school beat, such as football or baseball. Being on the football beat, for example, entails preparing game previews, covering games, keeping statistics, and doing features on players or teams. It also means picking up the phone and talking to coaches, just to find out what's going on. You never know when you might stumble onto something that turns out to be interesting.

AT A GLANCE

Salary Range

What you earn depends upon your experience and the size and location of the publication. Generally speaking, you can expect to make $15,000 a year as an entry-level sportswriter at a small paper, all the way up to more than $125,000 as an established sportswriter at a major city daily.

Education/Experience

An undergraduate degree, preferably in journalism, is a must. Also, the more you can write for your school newspapers in high school and college, the better. Another key is getting an internship with a daily newspaper.

Personal Attributes

It helps to be well read, inquisitive, a self-starter, and a good listener. You'll be dealing with athletes, coaches, and administrators a lot, asking questions and trying to get information. Being pleasant and persistent are qualities that should serve you well.

Requirements

Journalism degree.

Outlook

Newspaper circulation has declined as people's use of the Internet has skyrocketed. The glut of cable news, available at the touch of a remote control button, has also contributed to the decreasing popularity of newspapers. It's likely that more papers will increase their Internet content. But you'd need a crystal ball to determine what the future holds for the traditional newspaper. If you have your heart set on becoming a newspaper sportswriter, be prepared to work hard and have an ample supply of determination.

Covering games, no matter what the sport, means you'll have to interview players and coaches afterward. You'll want to ask questions that give your readers insight into what happened and why.

When it's time to write your story, whether you return to the office or file from the game site on your laptop, you'll always need to keep one eye on the clock, because newspaper deadlines are strict. If the deadline is midnight, getting your story finished at 12:01 isn't going to cut it.

Let's say your game ends at 10:45 p.m. It takes 15 minutes to interview the coaches and players in the locker room, and you're ready to start writing at 11. That leaves about 45 minutes to finish your story, because you have to allow time for it to be edited. You'll also have to allow for some time to do the box score. So that hour between 11 and midnight will be hectic and nerve-wracking, but the more experience you gain, the easier it will get. After awhile, you'll be able to deal with those situations without your hands shaking and your knees knocking.

What if you've grown up playing and watching baseball and football and basketball? You know, the sports that most people are familiar with. But your editor tells you that your beat will be track and field, and it so happens that you wouldn't know what a discus was if one hit you in the head.

It's up to you find out as much as you can about the sport. You'll have to educate yourself, so it all makes sense to your readers.

Not all of your stories will be game stories written on deadline. You'll have plenty of opportunities to write feature stories, concerning a person, an event, or an issue. These are enjoyable, because they are typically more in depth and less time sensitive. You'll have a chance to interview people at length and give your readers a real sense of the person or situation.

As you move up the ladder, the top rung would be covering a high-profile professional or college team. Those assignments usually go to the most experienced and talented sportswriters; those who have worked hard honing their craft and developing a writing style that is informative and entertaining.

You'll have the best seat in the house, in the press box, and if you're lucky, you'll be able to cover your team in a showcase event such as a bowl game, the World Series, or the Super Bowl.

And if you reach that top step of the ladder, you'll be able to look back at the grunt work you did in the beginning of your career and realize it was all worth it.

Pitfalls

There is no such thing as having regular hours while working for a newspaper. The job entails working nights, weekends, and holidays. It also involves irregular hours and a schedule that can change from week to week. If you have a beat that requires travel, that, too, can be a downside after awhile, unless you like waiting in airports. If you're not talented enough to land a job at a major city daily, you're not likely to get rich while working as a sportswriter, either.

Perks

You'll be around sports and games and athletes. You'll be able to tell interesting stories about exciting games and fascinating people. And if you work hard and move up the ladder, you'll be able to attend big-time events.

Get a Jump on the Job

Write every chance you get—for your high school paper, for your college paper, for your local paper as a stringer, if possible. Getting an internship at a daily newspaper is key, because it will allow you gain practical experience and compile a portfolio of clips that will go a long way in job interviews. Read as much as you can, taking notice of writing styles and how other writers do their jobs.

Jonathan Rand, sportswriter

When Jonathan Rand was a junior at Stuyvesant High School in New York City, he wasn't exactly tearing it up academically. He did okay, but Stuyvesant was a very competitive school, and Rand rarely found himself near the top of the class in any subject.

But one day his class received an assignment from Mr. Marks, his English teacher, to write an essay. Marks was a demanding teacher who was devoted to improving the quality of his students' writing.

When the grades came back, the kids who had been doing so well on physics and geometry tests had struggled on the essay. Rand, on the other hand, received one of the highest grades in the class.

It was about that time that a light bulb went off in Rand's mind.

"This made me realize that I had a talent for writing, and I already was interested in sports," he says. And from there, the rest is history. Rand became a sportswriter, eventually getting a job at the *Kansas City Star,* one of the most respected newspapers in the United States.

Rand's first assignment as a sportswriter was covering Stuyvesant football games for *The Spectator,* his high school newspaper. He continued his career in college at the State University of New York at Buffalo, where he majored in political science.

"I kept writing about sports," Rand says, "and it remained a hobby until I graduated and had to start figuring out my future. I decided the two things I liked best were sports and writing. So I figured it would be great if I could combine the two for a career. That's when I decided to take the plunge and pursue a master's in journalism [at the University of Missouri] with the idea of becoming a sportswriter."

Rand graduated from the Missouri School of Journalism in January 1970, after writing his thesis on the history of *The Morning Telegraph,* a newspaper devoted to horse racing, one of his longtime interests.

When it came time to go job-hunting, Rand wasn't overwhelmed with offers. In fact, his first job had nothing to do with sports. He went to work for *Cash Box,* a music magazine based in New York City.

It was nearly a year after he graduated from Missouri, December 1970, that he landed a job with the now-defunct *Miami News,* where he broadened his horizons by covering a variety of sports—University of Miami athletics, professional and amateur boxing, the Baltimore Orioles in spring training, minor league baseball, the Miami Dolphins, and pari-mutuel sports. In his spare time, he also wrote a column devoted to radio and TV.

After six years, he moved to the other newspaper in town, the still-thriving *Miami Herald,* where he covered University of Miami sports, Florida State sports, horse racing, golf, and the Dolphins.

As you can see, being versatile in your ability to cover a wide range of sports can be a tremendous advantage.

Rand's next stop was the *Kansas City Star* in November 1979. It was there he settled in as the beat writer for the Kansas City Chiefs. Instead of covering lots of different sports, he was able to devote most of his time and energy to one subject.

Being a beat writer, especially a new beat writer, can be a daunting responsibility. You have to familiarize yourself with a new town, a new team, new players, and new colleagues. But once he got his feet on the ground, Rand finally had some structure to his day.

(continues)

(continued)

A typical day began with arriving for practice and shooting the breeze with trainers, equipment managers, assistant coaches, or anyone who happened to be hanging around. "You do that to maintain a rapport and a presence and maybe get a lead on a news story," he says.

Forming those relationships can be valuable, because you're usually required to file a story every day, whether or not there's any earth-shattering news. If there's not, then your best bet is a feature story.

"You determine what the best feature story would be that day, and at the end of practice you interview your player and develop an angle," Rand says. "You try to add depth by also talking to the head coach, an assistant coach, teammates, etc."

Covering a major league baseball team is a little different, because you have access to players before each game, which necessitates the reporter to show up at the ballpark about three hours prior to the first pitch. Most papers require a pregame story, which can be a compilation of notes about the previous game, personnel moves or the state of the team. That story is filed early.

Once the game starts, especially if it's at night, reporters usually write a running account of the game so the story can be filed by deadline. Then it's back to the clubhouse to do interviews so you can update your story for later editions.

As you can see, there's a lot to do and deadline pressure to get it done—accurately and on time.

"But it's a job that affords you a certain degree of independence," Rand says. "And it gives you the chance to meet people who are at the top of their professions, whether they be athletes, managers, coaches, or general managers, and write about subjects in which you're interested."

Getting the chance to work for a major city daily newspaper and cover a professional or big-time college team on a regular basis requires a person that is a self-starter, not a clock watcher.

"Take the initiative when you can," Rand says, when asked what a key was to getting that first job. "Newspapers editors appreciate young people who are willing to take initiative. Finding that first job is always the hardest, but don't get discouraged. Writing and reporting skills are paramount. A good writer and reporter can always learn the ins and outs of a sport, but a former athlete or expert on a sport usually can't develop high-level writing and reporting skills."

There's another skill that's required once you land that job of your dreams. If you're assigned to be the beat person for a pro team, and you're getting to know the players on that team on a personal basis, remember: You're there to work, not star gaze.

"You're a journalist covering sports, not a sports fan with a press pass," Rand says. "Treat athletes like other news sources: with respect, not awe."

If you get too close to the team and its players, you'll be unable to be an effective reporter. Your job is to serve your readers, not please the players.

But if you're conscientious and work hard, there's a good chance you can do both. That's not to suggest that players will like or agree with everything you write, but if you're thorough, fair, and reasonable, it's likely that they will respect the fact that you have a job to do—even if the job you're doing can sometimes annoy them.

STADIUM VENDOR

OVERVIEW

Have you ever dreamed about getting paid to go to a ballgame or a rock concert? That's what vendors do, though they're bound to miss some plays or songs here and there while they're hiking up and down the stands, hawking food and drinks.

Stadium vendors work for a *concessionaire*—a company that holds a contract to sell food, drinks, souvenirs, programs, and yearbooks at a stadium or arena. If you've ever been to a ballgame and noticed hordes of hungry fans waiting in lines to buy hot dogs, peanuts, and beer, you know what a great business concessions are.

But because these events usually last just a few hours, it wouldn't make sense for concessionaires to hire full-time vendors—so their sales force works part time, for extra income. Because most sports and entertainment events are held during evenings or weekends, most vendors can work at these events without disrupting their full-time job. You'll find vendors who keep their job for just a few months, and others who stay for decades. Time on the job is important, because the vendors who get to sell the best products in the best locations are the ones with the most seniority.

Vendors who've been at their job for many years can count on working any event they want. They usually get to sell the most profitable items and work in the most expensive seating areas. But some vendors show up for work not certain of being hired. The concessionaire usually can guess how big a staff will be needed

AT A GLANCE

Salary Range
$2,000 to $50,000 annually.

Education/Experience
You don't need a college degree, though many students help pay their college tuition by working as a vendor during the summer. It helps to have experience in any kind of sales, especially to the public.

Personal Attributes
You need to have a loud voice and be willing to whoop and holler and call attention to yourself and your product. You should be friendly so customers will want to buy your items. You should be patient with fans who are slow deciding what they want or getting out their money. You need to be observant so you can see a customer trying to catch your attention. You should feel comfortable dealing with people from many different walks of life.

Requirements
You'll need to demonstrate you can comfortably lift the load you'll be asked to carry. To sell beer, wine, or liquor, you'll have to obtain a special license and be of legal drinking age in your state.

Outlook
As long as fans pack stadiums and arenas for sports and entertainment, there will be jobs for vendors. This is one job that won't be replaced by machines or the Internet. For many fans, buying from a vendor is part of the fun of watching a ballgame.

for an event based on the weather, advance sales, and ticket lines, but sometimes vendors don't find out they're not needed until after they report for roll call.

Once a vendor has been picked to work, it's off to the cash window to get change and put on a uniform, and then on to a commissary (the area where food and drink is stocked). The vendor picks up the first

Bob Reital, stadium beer and snack vendor

There you are, sitting in the stands cheering on your favorite team. Odds are you don't pay much attention to the guy running up and down the stands, lugging beer. But Bob Reital knows he's there to help you enjoy the game. You'll find him selling beer at Kansas City Royals games at Kauffman Stadium during the spring and summer and at Chiefs games at Arrowhead Stadium during fall and early winter.

Whether he's carrying trays of beer, hot dog warmers, or a pile of pretzels, he gets a strenuous workout—especially when he's trudging up and down steep steps on a steamy summer night. It's common to see stadium vendors dripping with sweat as they lug their items up and down the stadium. Reital once tried saving time on refills by carrying two cases of beer instead of one, but found that 48 bottles, the ice, and a tray were too heavy a load. "That'll kill you," he says. The loads feel heaviest at the start of the season. "You don't have to be Arnold Schwarznegger. When I started out, I thought there was no way I could do this. But you will build up to where you can." Reital has learned to be adaptable because he's held so many different jobs. He's delivered phone books, transported railroad crews, sacked groceries, installed cable TV, and cut lumber—until the day he answered a newspaper ad for stadium vendors in 2003 and was hired by Centerplate, the concessionaire for both Royals' and Chiefs' games. He had to get a special license to sell beer, usually a hot seller. "Some days it is, some days it isn't," he says philosophically. "Some days you're the windshield. Sometimes you're the bug."

Although he's usually hustling, Reital usually sees most of a baseball game. "Whether they're winning or losing, I love the atmosphere," he says. But his income does depend on whether the home team is winning or losing. When the Royals hit hard times, crowds fell off, and so did beer sales. The Chiefs, however, usually draw crowds of almost 80,000, and Reital can sell 10 cases of beer during a game. "Every day is a good day at a Chiefs' game," he says. However, a beer vendor has to remember when to stop selling. To cut down on the number of intoxicated fans who may be driving home, the Royals stop selling beer after the eighth inning and the Chiefs stop after the third quarter. Reital leaves the stands quickly so he doesn't have to argue with fans who might demand a beer after the deadline. He's also expected to refuse to serve any customer who appears to be drunk.

Reital knows he's going to have a good night at a baseball game when customers empty his first case of beer while he's still walking from the commissary to his section in the upper deck. He's also sold bottled water, soda, and peanuts, but couldn't get the hang of tossing a peanut bag. If a customer is seated in the middle of a row, the peanut vendor usually throws the bag like a baseball and the customer is supposed to catch it. " I sold peanuts once and smacked a guy in the face," Reital says. "I says: 'I'm not doing this anymore.' It's tough, especially when you can't pitch!"

batch of items and gives the commissary manager a ticket to account for the load, and then tries to get to the stands before the event starts.

Some vendors develop a distinctive selling style. By having a catch phrase, a rhyme or joke, or a sing-song way of hawking their product, vendors can become so popular that customers want to buy especially from them. Vendors, in that sense, are like any other salespeople. The most successful ones figure out how to separate themselves from the rest.

If there's a big crowd, vendors might sell their first batches of food or drinks quickly. On a slow night, it might seem like forever until they're sold out. Once the supply is empty, the vendor returns to the commissary for another load. At the end of the event, vendors turn in the money to a cash office and receive a commission for each item sold; they get a check after their receipts are totaled. They also may be eligible for a year-end bonus. (Employees at concession stands, however, are paid by the hour.)

Most vendors try to increase their income by working more than one type of event. Even a major league baseball team, which plays 162 games, is home only half the time between April and September, so a vendor might work several venues and for more than one concessionaire. In a city such as New York, Boston, or Chicago, a vendor might be able to choose among jobs for major league baseball, pro and college pro football, pro basketball, pro hockey, auto racing, concerts, and circuses.

Pitfalls

You're not always guaranteed work, and it can be exhausting carrying heavy trays or containers up and down steps, especially on a hot night. Vendors also have to deal with rude and intoxicated customers.

Perks

You can see a lot of great events for free while making extra income—all while still working at your full-time job. You can have some really good days if you're selling a popular product at a big football game or auto race drawing crowds of 80,000 or more.

Get a Jump on the Job

The next time you attend a stadium or arena event, take a first-hand look at what it's like to be a vendor. Observe them as they walk up and down the aisles and make their sales pitches. If you're of high school age, apply to a concessionaire for a job.

TEAM PHYSICIAN

OVERVIEW

They don't see any game action; their names and numbers aren't included on the roster in the game program; they don't even get uniforms, for goodness sakes. But they can be among the most important people to a team's success.

Injuries are part of the territory when it comes to athletics. No matter how well conditioned athletes are, they suffer injuries. That's why the team physician is a critical part of any sports program.

It doesn't matter if the injury is nagging or serious, the team physician can help get the players back where they belong—in the game and contributing to their team's success.

The overriding responsibility of the team physician is to treat the athletes on the team for their injuries, and then coordinate their subsequent medical care with the training staff and other doctors. It's important that everyone involved be on the same page so that an athlete's treatment and recovery take place as quickly as possible.

It goes without saying that any team physician should be very familiar with musculoskeletal injuries, be trained in CPR, and be able to administer emergency treatment. Some team physicians are medical doctors with specialized training in sports medicine; others are trained as surgeons, who have spent the last year of their education dedicated specifically to sports medicine.

Each professional team has its own head team physician, while a college or

AT A GLANCE

Salary Range

A team physician who isn't a surgeon can earn anywhere from $125,000 to $175,000 a year. A team physician with a surgical specialty can earn from $180,000 to $250,000 a year. College or university team physicians are paid less than physicians in private practice.

Education/Experience

Be prepared for a lot of school. First there's a four-year undergraduate degree, with grades good enough to get you into medical school. Should you choose to become a surgeon, that's an additional six years—five years of general orthopedics and one year specifically dedicated to sports medicine. If you choose a nonsurgical path, you'll have the four years of medical school, three years of post–medical school residency, and one year of fellowship.

Personal Attributes

Given the educational requirements, you'll obviously have to be a person who is hardworking and determined. Make that very hardworking and very determined. If you've chosen to go into sports medicine it's also a given that you would love sports.

Requirements

There are any number of organizations you can join and be certified by such as the American Orthopaedic Society for Sports Medicine, the American College of Sports Medicine, and the American Medical Society for Sports Medicine. These organizations provide continuing education opportunities to allow physicians to keep current with changes in the industry.

Outlook

If you can make it through the rigorous educational demands, the prospects for landing a job should be pretty good. Sports programs continue to expand in the United States, and the job market for team physicians should follow suit.

university is likely to have one head team physician to take care of the athletes in all of the school's sports. For high schools that employ team physicians, one doctor might take care of the athletes from several schools.

The team physician is involved in every aspect of an athlete's medical care, starting with the physical examination each athlete receives prior to the start of the season. He or she also takes care of injuries sustained

on the field, either in practice or games; coordinates the rehabilitation schedule; and has the primary input as to when the athlete is ready to return to action.

Team physicians have to be aware that athletes, because they are in such outstanding physical condition, may not take as long to recover as your normal video-game playing couch potato. So if the conventional medical wisdom holds that it takes eight weeks to recover from

Wayne J. Sebastianelli, M.D., team physician

The Big Ten football game between Ohio State and Penn State at Beaver Stadium in State College, Pennsylvania, on Saturday, Sept. 23, 2000, was a lot like any other game. The stadium was packed with fans, and the two teams were slugging it out in what has become a fierce rivalry between the two schools.

Then, suddenly, everything changed. Penn State's Adam Taliaferro, a freshman cornerback from Voorhees, New Jersey, tackled Jerry Westbrook, a 231-pound running back. Taliaferro's head collided with Westbrook's knee, causing Taliaferro's head to snap back violently. He landed on the crown of his head and lay motionless on the turf.

In no time at all, Dr. Wayne Sebastianelli, the director of sports medicine at Penn State, raced onto the field, along with other doctors on his staff. He removed Taliaferro's helmet and shoulder pads and immobilized his head and neck.

Taliaferro had burst the fifth cervical vertebra in his neck and bruised his spinal cord. He underwent decompression spinal fusion surgery Sept. 27, remained on a ventilator until Sept. 28, and then spent the next three months at Magee Rehabilitation Hospital in Philadelphia, near his South Jersey home. His rehab continued, rigorously, for most of the next year, and Sebastianelli continued to be involved in Taliaferro's treatment and recovery, flying from State College to Philadelphia nearly every weekend.

What looked like a dire, potentially fatal situation at the time of the injury turned out to be, as Sebastianelli put it, a "once-in-a-lifetime recovery." Nearly a year to the day after his injury, Taliaferro led the Penn State team onto the field for their home opener. And he didn't walk—he ran.

Sebastianelli was quoted in the press as saying: "I couldn't control my tears. It was one of the best feelings in the world to see a kid who was unable to do a thing for himself turn into someone who's going to be very, very functional. I had just a small role, but to be able to contribute to his overall well-being and recovery was really rewarding." Sebastianelli is being a bit modest when he describes his role as small, because Taliaferro and his family credit Sebastianelli, who acted quickly and expertly, with saving his life.

Such are the rewards of being a team physician. Obviously, you hope no athlete suffers such a serious injury, but if one occurs, you can see how important it is for the team physician to be able to meet the challenge.

a broken wrist, it shouldn't come as a surprise that some stud football player who's in terrific shape could be ready to play in six weeks.

Team physicians sometimes come under a lot of pressure from coaches to get players back on the field, especially the best players. It goes without saying that any coach wants his players—especially his best players—on the field and not on the sidelines in street clothes. So it's not unusual for a coach to do all he can to get the doctor to clear an injured player. And the coach isn't the only person who might exert pressure. The injured player himself might do what he can to convince the doctor to allow him back on the field. So it's important for the team physician to stand his ground and not clear players to return to action until their injuries are completely healed. Coaches and players might look at things in the short term, but it's

Sebastianelli played all sports as he was growing up, and he was skilled enough at football that he considered going to a Division I school to play. But instead, he chose the University of Rochester, because of its outstanding medical program. He played football at Rochester, middle guard on defense, and he suffered a few broken bones and a shoulder injury along the way. It was those injuries and their treatment that ultimately got him interested in orthopaedics. Who knows what career he might have chosen had he remained healthy throughout his college career?

Sebastianelli received his medical degree from the University of Rochester in 1983 and completed his residency in the Rochester area in 1988. From 1989 to 1992, he worked as an assistant professor of medicine within the Department of Orthopaedics at the University of Rochester School of Medicine and an associate surgeon at Monroe Community Hospital, also in Rochester.

He went to Penn State in 1992 as the first director of the Center for Sports Medicine, which is known as Penn State Orthopaedics. He became a tenured professor in 2003. His duties at Penn State include supervising and directing the medical care for athletes in the 29 NCAA Division I sports teams. He provides primary care, orthopaedic surgery, athletic training, physical therapy, and drug testing.

"A typical day on the job for me consists of a mix of seeing patients in the office; surgery; field or event coverage; and training room assessment," says Sebastianelli, who was named The Best Doctor in America in 2002. "This can involve up to approximately 50 patient and athlete encounters a day, or approximately eight to 10 hours of surgery a day. "Plus, I do travel to all events with the Penn State football team and to numerous events, especially during championship time with the basketball programs."

As you can see, the job of a team physician requires a lot of time and expertise. It also requires a great deal of education. To become a team physician with a surgical specialty, you have to make a huge commitment. Sebastianelli says you'll need a four-year undergraduate degree, followed by four years of medical school, followed by six years of orthopaedic training (five years of general training, one year of sports medicine experience). That adds up to 14 years of school after high school.

"Obviously, that is not a cup of tea for a lot of people," he says. But if it happens to be the "cup of tea" for you, Sebastianelli offers this bit of advice: "I would ask people to be committed to medicine first and then athletics second. You should always view your skill as being applied to the athlete and to a specific sport, but you have to be a physician first and a team physician second."

the team physician's responsibility to look long term and to consider, first and foremost, the player's health. It won't do the player, the coach or the team any good, if the player comes back early, only to suffer a reoccurrence of the same injury.

When it comes to medical matters and the well-being of the players, it's the team physician, not the head coach, who's in charge. Who knew a doctor could hold such a powerful position?

In addition to treating athletes for injuries and supervising their training and rehab, the team physician is responsible for educating the athletes, coaches, administrators' and the athletes' parents, if applicable, about the procedures that will be followed in case of injury; for establishing a chain of command among the staff; for planning and training for emergencies; and for ensuring proper event coverage by staff members.

Pitfalls

The road to becoming a team physician involves a whole lot of schooling and a whole lot of training. For instance, if you choose to become a team physician with a surgical specialty, you're looking at 14 years beyond high school. That's a long, long time before you land the job of your dreams.

Perks

If you make it through the years of education, the satisfaction alone of having persevered and succeeded should be enough to keep you going for years. There's also the chance to work with motivated athletes and help them be the best they can be.

Get a Jump on the Job

Know what you're getting yourself in for, educationally. Getting experience by working on the staff of the athletic trainer at your high school or college will help you gain valuable experience.

TENNIS PRO

OVERVIEW

If you love the *thwack* that a perfectly struck tennis ball makes when it flies off the racket strings, if you enjoy being with people, and if you're a skilled player, then a career as a tennis pro might be for you.

Being a tennis pro allows you to play a game that you love, and get paid for doing it, which is a pretty attractive combination for anyone looking for just the right job.

The first step in becoming a successful tennis pro is being a good player. These days, most pros are accomplished players, who have played United States Tennis Association (USTA) junior events, as well as high school and college tennis. Some instructors have even taken a shot at the professional ranks.

But playing tennis well and having the ability to teach tennis effectively are not one and the same. You could be the second coming of Pete Sampras or Steffi Graf, but if you don't have the people skills and the teaching techniques necessary, you probably won't be all that busy.

So it's important that you learn all you can about what makes a successful teacher. You can do that by taking lessons from some experienced pros, not so they can improve your game, but so that you can go to school on their teaching methods. There are also a slew of instructional books on the market that would prove helpful.

A key to becoming an excellent teacher is having the ability to play different styles of tennis. If you're most comfortable playing an aggressive, attacking style, using a powerful serve, that's great if all your students are looking to play the same way.

AT A GLANCE

Salary Range

What you'll make varies, depending upon the marketplace, your experience, and where you teach. If you're an assistant pro in a municipal recreation facility, you might earn as little as $10 an hour. If you are a head professional, teaching at a club or at a city park, you can expect to charge about $40 an hour for a lesson, with a small percentage going back to the employer. If you work at a country club, then your earning ability goes up. Clubs often pay their pros a monthly retainer, benefits, and mostly all of their income from lessons and pro shop sales. In a situation like that, an experienced pro can expect to earn in the neighborhood of $100,000 annually.

Education/Experience

A successful tennis pro should have a solid playing background. That means playing junior tennis, perhaps going on to play in college, and maybe even taking a shot at the pro ranks. Accepting an apprenticeship or internship with an established tennis pro is also a good idea. If you plan to be the director of tennis at a club, where you will also be expected to run the pro shop, knowing how to run and market a business is a must.

Personal Attributes

You could be a great player and a terrific teacher, but if you don't have a friendly, easygoing personality, you won't get a lot of students. You'll also need a fair amount of patience, because students progress at different rates and some will need more time on a particular skill than others. And being able to put into words what you want your students to do on the court will make your job—and their learning experience—a lot easier.

Requirements

If you want to be taken seriously as a tennis pro, you should get certified by the United States Professional Tennis Association (USPTA) or the

(continues)

AT A GLANCE *(continued)*

Professional Tennis Registry (PTR), which is more international in scope. There's no law that says you have to be certified in order to be a teaching pro, but being involved with these organizations allows you to keep up to date with the changes in the industry.

Outlook

Tennis participation in the United States has been flat over the last several years. But the United States Tennis Association has set a goal of 30 million players by 2010, an increase of about 5 million players. If that goal is reached, the job market for tennis pros should brighten.

But what if you have a student whose serve isn't strong enough to puncture a soap bubble, and who would rather tiptoe through traffic on the interstate than charge forward to the net?

Well, your big game style isn't going to be worth much to that student. So you've got to be prepared to teach all styles; you've also got to resist the temptation to force students to play a style that suits you, the instructor, better than it suits the student.

You'll also have to be able to explain more than just how to hit a forehand or a backhand, or the proper technique for developing a reliable serve. For example, there are the rules of the game; the scoring system, which is more complicated than most sports; and the strategy involved. Here's another instance where it's really important that you have good communication skills.

Another step on your road to becoming a tennis pro is getting certified. No, it's not required but yes, it's important (very important), because it adds to your credibility. Most high profile tennis camps and

resorts probably won't let you through the door unless you've been certified by one of two major organizations—the United States Professional Tennis Association (USPTA) or the Professional Tennis Registry (PTR).

Certification offers benefits to instructors such as courses and workshops on teaching tennis, liability insurance, specialized books and videos available only to members, job listings, subscriptions to tennis magazines including an exclusive members' magazine discounts on tennis merchandise, help with the business end of the profession, hosting for a Web site you create to promote your teaching, and eligibility for tournament competition against fellow members.

To get certified, you'll need to pass a test that could include demonstrating your own proficiency at executing various strokes, teaching a group and a private lesson, analyzing stroke errors, demonstrating grips, and passing a written exam that covers a wide range of tennis topics, including teaching, playing, equipment, and history.

The membership dues for each organization are worth it. Belonging to the USPTA or the PTR, not only gives your resume a boost in stature, but it allows you to keep up to date with changes in the industry.

You could end up teaching tennis on the courts at your local playground, at a swanky resort in a vacation hot spot, or some place in between. But no matter where you teach, be prepared to encounter a wide variety of students, who have a wide range of abilities.

Some of your lessons might be one-on-one. These private lessons are usually the highest-paying and are taught by the most experienced instructors. Small group lessons, with as many as six or eight students

Ron Woods, tennis pro

Had Ron Woods' parents not owned a grocery store in Corpus Christi, Texas, when he was growing up, and had they not had a rule requiring their kids to be active—or else—who knows whether he would've made being a tennis instructor his livelihood.

But he did, and it was that store and their rule that allowed him to be introduced to tennis.

"My parents had a rule that if you were not involved in some constructive activity—sports, hobbies, etc., that I would have to work in the store," Woods says. "Well, I made it a point to stay involved in as many activities as possible to not have to work in the store."

Woods did just about everything while he was in elementary school—baseball, football, track and field. When he entered junior high school, his dream was to continue playing football. But size-wise, he didn't cut it: He was too small. "So when I heard that there was a tennis team working out in the fall, I went out and tried for the team," he says.

The coach at Wynne Seale Junior High was Mary K. Wright, a phys ed teacher.

"She was a great teacher and coach," Woods says. "She encouraged me to play and helped me with the basics of the game. I fell in love with tennis and began to play every day that I could."

Woods played so often and so well through high school that he was awarded a tennis scholarship to the University of Houston.

While in college, Woods worked part time at the McGregor Park Tennis Center in Houston and at the HEB Tennis Center in Corpus Christi. After graduating from college in 1965, he was hired as an assistant tennis pro at HEB Tennis Center, working for Bob Mapes.

"I learned not only how to teach the game, but how to run the various programs involved with tennis, such as leagues, tournaments, and social mixers," Woods says. "I also learned quite a bit about how to run and manage a tennis pro shop, involving inventory, sales, display, and dealing with people."

Woods learned his lessons well, because after four years at HEB, he moved on to become the director of tennis at the Corpus Christi Country Club, where he developed a successful tennis program and retail shop.

How successful? Well, Woods spent 31 years at Corpus Christi Country Club, retiring in 2002.

His days as a tennis pro tended to be long, often starting at 7:30 a.m. and not ending until 9 p.m. When he wasn't teaching lessons, he was catching up with paperwork and dealing with the business aspect of the club.

"It takes long hours to be successful," he says. "But you can adjust the hours to take of family duties and still provide the services required of the country club business."

The best part of those hours on the job was spent on the court teaching.

"I loved working with my students; I really enjoyed teaching tennis," he says. "No matter what level of ability, I was always encouraging them to have fun and work hard to improve."

Woods, who has been on the national board of directors for the USPTA, strongly suggests getting certified by the organization, which will help them stay current in an industry that changes rapidly.

"I would also tell them to work hard on their game, to improve their own skills, and to study everything they can pertaining to the game," he says. "Also, go to work for a person who is successful, as you will learn so many things just from watching and helping to run a successful program.

"I would also tell a person interested in becoming a teaching pro to remember that this is a service industry and you must always find ways to keep your customers happy."

per instructor, are also an option. But what if you're called on to conduct a clinic for kids, all of whom are beginners? Well, if you want to avoid chaos, you'll need patience, organizational skills, and an instructional program designed to keep everyone busy and involved.

Pitfalls

Being a tennis pro can involve long hours, not just on the court, but taking care of all the non-tennis stuff, such as running the pro shop, if you're at a club or resort; organizing tournaments and special programs; and marketing the facility. Also, if you're interested in improving your own game, don't count on it. The more you teach, the less time you'll have to play.

Perks

You're helping your students learn a game that you love; you'll more than likely be able to develop your own lesson plan and teaching style; and you'll be paid for it. What could be better?

Get a Jump on the Job

Try to assist an established teaching pro. Even if the money isn't anything to get excited about, the experience you'll gain will pay off down the road. You can also try to get a job with your local recreation department, many of which have summer tennis programs.

TENNIS REFEREE

OVERVIEW

In general terms, the job of a tennis referee is to supervise all aspects of a tournament, making sure everything runs smoothly and everyone—players, umpires, linesmen, etc.—are where they're supposed to be when they're supposed to be there.

That said, the job of a tennis tournament referee actually starts before the tournament does. Once appointed by the tournament committee, the referee receives the list of entrants. His first responsibility is to make the tournament draw. A tennis draw sheet looks a lot like the bracket sheet for the NCAA basketball tournament. Each player is entered on a line of the draw sheet and advances to meet the person on the line above or below.

Once the draw is set, the referee is responsible for setting the schedule of matches and assigning the courts on which each match will be played.

Scheduling is sometimes regarded as an art form, because it's up to the referee to use the courts as efficiently as possible and make sure there is little or no down time between the end of one match and the start of another. You could say it's like putting together a huge jigsaw puzzle, except the referee uses the players as pieces.

Once the schedule is set and the tournament is ready to begin, the referee should meet with the deputy referee and the rest of the officials to make sure everyone is on the same page as far as the rules are concerned and that any penalties are assessed properly. The referee also has to assign the on-court officials to their matches, and in a pro tournament that means a chair umpire and six lines persons for each match. So

AT A GLANCE

Salary Range

Your salary will depend on the level of matches you are supervising, either local, national, or international. But once you become certified to work internationally as a referee, you can expect to make about $2,500 a week.

Education/Experience

You don't need a college degree to become a tennis referee, but you do need to be trained and certified by either the United States Tennis Association (USTA), the International Tennis Federation (ITF), and/or the Intercollegiate Tennis Association (ITA).

Personal Attributes

You'll need to be organized and detail-oriented, because a lot of what happens at a tennis tournament will be under your control and supervision. The tournament referee has a wide range of duties. You'll also have to be blessed with common sense, an analytical mind, and thick skin, because one of your major responsibilities will be to rule on disputes.

Requirements

In addition to being certified by the USTA, ITF, or ITA, referees also have to pass an annual test given by a USTA trainer-evaluator on either the sectional or national level. This annual certification is important, because it keeps referees up to date on rules changes or modifications and it allows for discussions of effective procedures for running tournaments.

Outlook

According to USTA rules, every sanctioned tournament must have a referee—and there are a lot of sanctioned tournaments as the USTA runs championships throughout the country for everyone from kids to seniors. So if you get the proper certification, chances are you'll be able to land a job. The job market, not surprisingly, is probably a bit tougher as you move up the ladder to the men's and women's pro tours and the Grand Slam tournaments.

Stefan Fransson, tennis referee

Generally speaking, the referee of a tennis tournament is content to remain behind the scenes, taking care of the many duties in relative privacy and running the event anonymously, at least as far as the fans are concerned.

Every now and then, there are times when the referee is forced to go public, in a manner of speaking. And when that happens, it's usually because there's a problem—in some cases, a big problem—on court between two players; a problem that can't be settled by the chair umpire.

So out comes the referee to render a decision and end the controversy. Stefan Fransson has been a tournament referee—his official title is that of supervisor—for some 20 years. He was on the scene during the 2003 French Open when Justine Henin-Hardenne and Serena Williams got involved in a dustup about whether a serve by Williams should have been allowed to be replayed. It got pretty ugly, with Williams accusing Henin-Hardenne of "lying and fabricating."

The controversy escalated to a point that Fransson was called on court by the chair umpire. He ultimately ruled in favor of Henin-Hardenne's version of events, and she went on to win the match in three sets.

Fransson was at a bit of a disadvantage having to deal with that controversy and many others like it.

"The most difficult part (of ruling on disputes) is that in most cases, I have not seen what really happened," he explains. "Most calls (to settle a dispute) come when you are working on another court or in the office."

Too bad he can't be everywhere at once, but because he can't be he has to take each player at their word and consider input from the chair umpire in order to render a ruling.

Not even that is the most trying part of his job as a peacemaker.

"The most difficult decisions to make are when players have done something wrong without intending to do so," Fransson says. "For example, in frustration and without looking, a player hits a ball which ends up hurting somebody, either a ball boy or ball girl, a line umpire, or a spectator. The rule in that situation is (the player) getting defaulted."

And then Fransson might be looked at as the bad guy, even though he was following the rules like he is supposed to.

Not all of Fransson's duties involve players who are upset. It's the referee's job to supervise all aspects of a tournament, including making the draw, scheduling matches, scheduling chair umpires and officials, assigning the courts, and deciding when play should be suspended due to weather or darkness. He has to exhibit leadership, organization, and the ability to communicate effectively.

Fransson began working as a referee when he was 17 years old. He officiated at national junior events in his native Sweden. In the early 1980s, he began working internationally, and then became a full-time supervisor in 1986.

the scheduling alone could be considered a full-time job.

When the matches begin, the referee is in charge of adjusting the schedule, because of inclement weather or matches that run longer than expected. It's also up to the ref to determine whether play should be suspended because of weather or darkness.

The climb up the ladder starts at the local level, which in this country would be the United States Tennis Association (USTA). Candidates are certified as provisional referees, sectional referees, USTA referees, national referees, and finally professional referees. To move up to the next classification of referee, you have to pass a test and accumulate more tournament experience than the previous step required.

For instance, a professional referee shall have attended school and passed the appropriate test, and shall have served as the referee in five tournaments, all of which were USTA National Championships, ITF International Championships, intercollegiate national tournaments, or professional tournaments with prize money of at least $10,000.

As you can see, the USTA is very picky about the requirements to become a referee, but that also goes to show what an important job it is.

The next level of certification, Fransson says, is done by the International Tennis Federation (ITF). Level 2 certification goes to officials that passed a written exam and practical exercise. They are known as ITF White Badge Officials.

Level 3 referees are advanced and are eligible to officiate at international matches, including the Grand Slam events, Davis Cup, Fed Cup, and the Olympics. They must pass a combination of written, oral, and on-court examinations before earning their certification.

Fransson is one of nine professional officials that are employed by the ITF. His specialty is rules and regulations.

A typical day for Fransson when he's working at an event starts about two hours before the matches begin. This allows him to make sure everything and everyone is ready for that day's play. Once play begins, he watches as many matches as possible, and he also handles scheduling, fines for code violations, and drug testing. Usually at the four Grand Slam events (Australian Open, French Open, Wimbledon, and the U.S. Open) there are as many as four supervisors, at least during the first week, to carry out all the responsibilities. The Grand Slam events are the most significant of the year; they last for two weeks and have men, women, juniors, and seniors playing at the same site.

As you might expect, the travel involved in Fransson's job can be both a blessing and a curse.

"After 20 years as a supervisor, it is still a bit difficult when the trips take you away from home for periods that are too long," he says. "Sometimes I'm on the road for three weeks or more in a row."

"But liking tennis as I do, it's obviously a great job. It's nice to work with a lot of different people from around the world."

As for advice to kids who think they'd like to make being a tennis referee a career, Fransson suggests contacting your local or national association and taking some courses.

"Then get out there and try it," he says. "See if you like it."

Part of the scheduling puzzle also includes making sure the playing field is level for everyone. In other words, if Player A and Player B are scheduled to meet at 10 a.m. Thursday, it would be best to avoid a situation where Player A's previous match ended at 3 p.m. Wednesday, but Player B's previous match didn't end until

9 p.m. It's important to make sure one player doesn't get an unfair advantage.

Another part of a referee's job is settling disputes. Usually, that can be handled by the chair umpire, who has the authority to overrule calls by the lines persons, assess point penalties, and make determinations on facts such as whether a ball was in or out, whether a player committed a double-hit, or whether a player committed a foot fault while serving.

But when one or both players refuse to heed the chair umpire's rulings or there is a disagreement on the interpretation of a rule, the referee has the final word. This is especially true in pro tournaments when the disputes become heated and the chair umpire's ruling is questioned.

As a rule of thumb, if you're watching a tournament on television and the referee makes an appearance on the court, you know that there were some fireworks preceding that arrival. The referee's word on the situation is final, and if warranted, the referee can go so far as to disqualify a player whose behavior warrants it.

So as you can see, the referee of a tennis tournament has many responsibilities to fulfill to ensure that the event runs smoothly. Perhaps the most important part of a referee's job is his presence. It's crucial that the referee be at the tournament site all the time, except for meals and other short breaks. When the referee is not able to be present, then it's up to him or her to make sure the deputy referee is there to fill in.

Pitfalls

The travel can be draining, especially if you are working as an international referee on one of the pro tours. It's not unusual for a referee to be away for several weeks at a time, which is difficult if you have a family or hate sitting in airports.

Perks

The travel can also be a benefit in that you might have the opportunity to visit new places and meet people from different countries and cultures. You also get to be around a sport you obviously have a passion for.

Get a Jump on the Job

Try to start by serving as a lines person or chair umpire on the local level to get experience in dealing with officiating a match. Volunteering at tournaments would give you the chance to see what goes into running an event in terms of scheduling and logistics. Also familiarize yourself with the rules of tennis and the point penalty system.

ZAMBONI DRIVER

OVERVIEW

Although ice resurfacing machines have become known almost universally as Zambonis or Zamboni machines, "Zamboni" is actually a brand name of a particular ice resurfacing machine. It's sort of like calling a tissue a "Kleenex," or a copy photo a "Xerox." A Kleenex is a brand of tissues, and a Xerox is a brand of copy machine. A Zamboni driver, then, would more correctly be called an ice resurfacing machine driver—except nobody does, so we won't, either.

Frank Zamboni invented the ice resurfacing machine back in the 1940s. It turns out that Zamboni owned a huge ice skating rink, and didn't like how much time it took to clean and resurface the ice. So he invented the Zamboni machine, which basically shaves off a thin layer of ice to smooth it out, and then releases a coating of water to resurface the ice. That was the original technology then, and with a lot of refinements and improvements, it remains the technology today.

There are about 10 different Zamboni models, along with other brands of ice resurfacing machines, most of which weigh between 5,000 and 6,000 pounds and cost somewhere in the neighborhood of $55,000.

Operating the Zamboni usually falls under the responsibility of the building operations crew, which also is normally responsible for general upkeep and maintenance of the arena.

The National Hockey League requires that two machines resurface the ice before the game, after warm-ups, between periods, during playoffs, and when the game ends. Many smaller arenas also use two machines.

While it may look sort of like just driving around a big tractor, it takes some practice to get used to driving a

Dan Strawhecker, Zamboni driver

Technically, Dan Strawhecker is not a Zamboni driver. Technically, he's an ice resurfacing machine driver who happens to drive a machine manufactured by a Canadian company called Olympia. You could call him an "Olympia driver," but then nobody would know what the heck you were referring to.

Strawhecker works as a member of the building operations department at a minor league hockey arena in Hershey, Pennsylvania, home of the Hershey Chocolate Company, a very popular amusement park, a first-class hotel and resort, and a concert arena.

While Strawhecker enjoys many aspects of his job, he's always glad when it's his turn to get behind the wheel of the ice resurfacer. "It's gotten to be a little bit routine, but it's still fun to drive the machine," Strawhecker says. "Little kids will wave and shout at you. I guess kids are fascinated by all big machines, but they sure do like this one."

The ice resurfacer operates much like a car does, Strawhecker says, so it's not overly difficult to drive. He and other drivers are required to study the manual and watch videos that detail its operation.

"It's important to understand how it works so that you can keep it maintained and running at its best," Strawhecker says.

You also need to remember that you're driving on ice, he says, and sometimes prone to slipping.

"It's like driving in the snow," Strawhecker says. "It's slippery, and you need to remember that. It's not like you can get going very fast, because the machine doesn't go more than about eight miles an hour. But you've got to watch on the turns. I was working with somebody once who ran into the boards and tore them up a little bit."

Strawhecker recommends that if you're interested in getting into arena building operations, you should get any type of job at a rink or arena that you can, and observe how the arena operates. Work hard, advance through the ranks, and then move on to a larger facility. Before you know it, you'll be driving a Zamboni for a major league hockey team.

some practice to get used to driving a Zamboni. The ice is slippery, and although the machine has special tires, it's still prone to sliding around, especially during turns.

Although most hockey fans don't object to watching the Zamboni at work, the fact is that they've really come to watch hockey, so there's some pressure on the Zamboni driver to get on and off the ice as quickly as possible, so that the game can continue. Two machines can do the job in about three minutes; with just one machine, it takes between six and seven minutes to resurface the ice.

Kids have a special fascination with Zambonis and other ice resurfacing machines, and so the job of Zamboni driver has received a good deal of attention over the years. At some arenas, Zamboni drivers get almost as much attention as the players do.

Pitfalls

Most hockey games are played at night, and can go pretty late if there's a late start or the game goes into overtime. If you like banker's hours, that could present a problem.

In addition, there aren't a lot of jobs out there; there are only so many Zambonis around, so only a limited number of people are needed to drive them. And, if you get nervous when you have to be in front of a lot of people, you might want to rethink your job plans. The ice resurfacing machines for some reason capture the imagination and interest of hockey fans, many of whom enjoy watching them do their things during breaks in the hockey action. That means that a lot of attention is on the driver.

Perks

If you love being in front of a crowd, then read the information in the previous section and consider it a big perk, rather than a pitfall. Add to that getting to hang out with hockey players and watching hockey games as part of your job, and draw your own conclusions.

Get a Jump on the Job

If you're interested in being a Zamboni driver, you'll need to develop some mechanical ability by reading, taking some technical courses, and getting hands-on experience by working on engines and machinery. If there's a stadium or arena in your area—even a small one—get a part-time job there when you're old enough, just to get a feel for what arena work entails. If there's a hockey rink near you, try to get any sort of work there that you can, and then pay attention to how the rink is run and what is involved in its upkeep.

APPENDIX A. ASSOCIATIONS, ORGANIZATIONS, AND WEB SITES

ATHLETIC DIRECTOR, HIGH SCHOOL

National Association of Collegiate Directors of Athletics
PO Box 16428
Cleveland, OH 44116
(440) 892-4000
http://www.nacda.collegesports.com

Founded in 1965, the National Association of Collegiate Directors of Athletics (NACDA) provides educational and networking opportunities for its 6,100 individual members. About 1,600 colleges and universities are represented by the NACDA. It holds an annual conference at which relevant problems affecting the administration arm of athletics are addressed, and sponsors clinics and workshops for its members.

BOXER

International Female Boxers Association
50B Peninsula Center Drive, #120
Rolling Hills Estates, CA 90274
(310) 428-1402
info@ifba.com
http://www.ifba.homestead.com

The International Female Boxers Association was formed in 1997 to promote the sport of boxing for women. The organization sponsors matches in various parts of the world. Its Web site has links to other boxing sites and provides news about matches and female boxers. It also offers advice on finding a trainer, a good gym, and equipment.

North American Boxing Organization
22937 Arlington Avenue, Suite 203
Torrance, CA 90501
(310) 517-0135
boxing@wbo-int.com
http://www.wbo-int.com

The North American Boxing Organization is a division of the World Boxing Organization and shares its Web site. The non-profit organization was established to promote the sport of boxing, establish rules at the professional level, and serve as an authoritative voice in issues concerning the sport. The organization's extensive site provides boxing news, real time coverage of matches, rules and regulations, standings, and much more.

BOXING TRAINER

North American Boxing Organization
22937 Arlington Avenue, Suite 203
Torrance, CA 90501
(310) 517-0135
boxing@wbo-int.com
http://www.wbo-int.com

The North American Boxing Organization is a division of the World Boxing Organization and shares its Web site. The non-profit organization was established to promote the sport of boxing, establish rules at the professional level, and serve as an authoritative voice in issues concerning the sport. The organization's extensive site provides boxing news, real time coverage of matches, rules and regulations, standings, and much more.

BULL RIDER

**The Professional Rodeo Cowboys
  Association (PRCA)**
101 ProRodeo Drive
Colorado Springs, CO 80919
(719) 593-8840
http://prorodeo.org/

*The Professional Rodeo Cowboys
Association (PRCA) is the largest and oldest
rodeo organization in the world. Almost
700 PRCA-sanctioned rodeos are held each
year, paying out over $34 million.*

Professional Bull Riders, Inc.
6 South Tejon Street, Suite 700
Colorado Springs, CO 80903
(719) 471-3008
http://www.pbrnow.com/

*Unlike traditional rodeo associations,
Professional Bull Riders, Inc. is dedicated
to making bull riding a stand-alone
sport. The PBR tour includes 29 cities
and $10 million in prizes*

RodeoAttitude.com
http://www.rodeoattitude.com

*This huge site is dedicated to all things
rodeo, including information about
associations, events, breeders, arenas, and
other rodeo sources. You'll also find links
to more information about each individual
rodeo event (including bull riding) and links
to the homepages of many rodeo personnel
and athletes. You can even connect with
other rodeo fans and professionals through
message boards and forums.*

**Women's Professional Rodeo Association
  (WPRA)**
1235 Lake Plaza Drive Suite 127
Colorado Springs, CO 80906
(719) 576-0900
http://www.wpra.com

*While many people think of bull riding
and other rodeo events as a "guy-thing,"
many women can and do compete in
rodeo events, including bull riding.*

DRAG RACER

National Hot Rod Association
2035 Financial Way
Glendora, CA 91741
(626) 914-4761
http://www.nhra.com

*Founded in 1951 by a man named Wally
Parks, the National Hot Rod Association
(NHRA) was originally formed as a means
of getting drag racers off the streets and
onto legal tracks. Today, the organization
has more than 80,000 members and
35,000 licensed competitors, and is the
world's largest promoter of professional
drag racing. The NHRA has 140 member
tracks in seven zones across the United
States on which weekly competitions are
held. Many of the tracks offer a junior
drag racing program that gives young
people who are between eight and 17 a
chance to drive half-scale dragsters in a
controlled setting. The NHRA Web site
provides lots of information about drag
racing, racers, terms of drag racing, and
links to other sites.*

GOLF BALL DIVER

**Professional Association of Diving
  Instructors**
30151 Tomas Street
Rancho Santa Margarita, CA 92688-2125
webmaster@padi.com
http://www.padi.com

*The Professional Association of Diving
Instructors is a worldwide organization that
promotes the instruction of scuba diving
and snorkeling at all levels. It focuses on
the safety of all divers, and works to raise
awareness of how important proper training
is for people wanting to learn to dive. Its
certification program is one of the best*

known and respected worldwide. Training is available at many different levels for all ages.

GOLF CADDIE

PCA Worldwide, Inc.
Professional Caddies Association
23 Malacompra Road
Palm Coast, FL 32137
(386) 446-8721
pca@pcaworldwide.com
http://www.pcaworldwide.com

PCA Worldwide, Inc. is an association founded for the benefit of professional golf caddies. The association offers a self-study course on how to become a professional caddie, and works to find additional educational and income opportunities for its members. Its Web site provides links to numerous other sites relating to golf and caddying.

GOLF COURSE ARCHITECT

American Society of Golf Course Architects
125 N. Executive Drive, Suite 106
Brookfield, WI 53005
(262) 786-5960
info@asgca.org
http://www.golfdesign.org

The American Society of Golf Course Architects (ASGCA) was founded in 1946. Its members are actively involved with designing and building new golf courses or redesigning older courses. Members must have at least eight years of job experience. The ASGCA works to assure that golf course design is done in a manner that is environmentally responsible, and is involved with many issues related to the game and profession of golf. The ASGCA is a good source of information about golf course

design, with examples of outstanding design and featured golf course architects.

GOLF PRO

The Professional Golf Association of America
100 Avenue of the Champions
Palm Beach Gardens, FL 33418
(800) 618-5535
http://www.pga.com

The Professional Golf Association of America (PGA) was founded in 1916 and has grown into the world's largest sports organization. The PGA, which works to educate people about the game of golf and its benefits, has more than 28,000 members. Its Web site is huge, offering everything from TV golf schedules to tips on improving your game. There's also a section for junior golfers, notes on various types of golf equipment, statistics of professional players participating in the PGA tour, and much more.

GOLF TOURNAMENT DIRECTOR

United States Golf Association
PO Box 708
Far Hills, NJ 07931
(908) 234-2300
http://www.usga.org

The United States Golf Association was founded in 1894 to serve as the national governing body for golf. The non-profit organization sponsors a variety of programs to enhance all levels of golf, and offers a members program for individuals who wish to support the sport of golf. The association is responsible for writing the rules and regulations that pertain to golf, and it sponsors 13 national championships each year. Its Web site provides reports on golf equipment, information about the rules of golf, and more.

GRAND PRIX DRESSAGE RIDER

American GrandPrix Association
1301 Sixth Avenue West, Suite 406
Bradenton, FL 34205
http://www.stadiumjumping.com/aga/index.cfm

The AGA promotes Olympic-caliber show jumping in the United States.

HOCKEY PLAYER

The National Hockey League
1251 Avenue of the Americas, 47th Floor
New York, NY 10020
(212) 789-2000
http://www.nhl.com

The National Hockey League (NHL) was organized in Canada in 1917, and is one of four major pro sports associations in North America. In addition to 30 major league teams, the NHL represents five minor and semi-pro hockey leagues. The organization establishes and enforces rules, collects licensing fees for merchandise, helps teams to negotiate broadcast fees, and regulates team ownership. Its Web site offers fantasy games, special features for kids and students, hockey news, standings, job listings, and much more.

MINOR LEAGUE GENERAL MANAGER

Minor League Baseball
201 Bayshore Drive, S.E.
St. Petersburg, FL 33701
(727) 822-6937
webmaster@minorleaguebaseball.com
http://www.minorleaguebaseball.com

Minor League Baseball (MLB) was founded in 1901 as the National Association of Professional Baseball Leagues. It promotes and oversees minor league baseball. The MLB is an extremely active organization, both during baseball season and in the off season. It sponsors an annual job fair, promotional seminar, baseball trade shows, winter meetings, and more. Its Web site is extensive, providing information for fans, players, managers, umpires, and other employees.

PERSONAL FITNESS TRAINER

National Federation of Professional Trainers
PO Box 4579
Lafayette, IN 47903
(800) 729-6378
http://nfpt.com

The National Federation of Professional Trainers (NFPT) was founded in 1988 to offer standardized training and certification for professional trainers. The NFPT has committees that study training methods and industry trends and set standards for the certification of trainers. Members of the organization can participate in continuing education and have the benefit of networking with other trainers. The NFPT Web site provides links to other sites that address issues relating to personal training.

PIT CREW MEMBER

National Association of Pit Crew Members
http://www.off-road.com/race/crews/napcm

An organization recognizing the efforts of racing pit crew and team members and the contribution that they make to their field.

RACEHORSE GROOM

Groom Elite Program
4063 Iron Works Parkway, B2
Lexington, KY 40511

(859) 321-4552

http://www.thehorsemeneliteprogram.com

The Groom Elite Program mission is to provide grooms an opportunity for professional and personal growth, by increasing their understanding of the horse with which they work and enhancing their professional skills. The course is taught at the track, during the track's dark days and is free of charge to the licensed personnel. The curriculum was developed by college professors who are equine and racing experts with the assistance of industry experts. It is targeted to racing, designed to be dynamic and very hands-on. The 30-hour course is designed to fill in many of the gaps in knowledge and understanding that long time backstretch workers may have while laying down a foundation for newer workers. The classroom portion of the program is supplemented with computer-generated slide shows rich with photos and illustrated examples of what is being discussed.

SCOREBOARD OPERATOR

Stadium Managers Association

(515) 282-8192, ext. 201

sma@assoc-mgmt.com

http://www.stadiummanagers.org

Formed in 1974, SMA promotes the professional, efficient, and state-of-the-art management of stadiums around the world. Its members are administrators, operators, and marketing personnel from teams, government entities, colleges and universities, and suppliers to the industry.

SNOWBOARD INSTRUCTOR

United States of America Snowboard Association

PO Box 3927

Truckee, CA 96160

(800) 404-9213

karen@usasa.org

http://www.usasa.org

The United States of America Snowboard Association (USASA) was founded in 1988 as a governing body for competitive snowboarding. The USASA sponsors varying levels of competition, including a national championship. The organization's Web site provide links to hundreds of competitions divided by region, making it easy for members to find competitive events in their areas. The site also provides a member message board and links to other snowboarding sites.

SPORTS AGENT

Sports Management Worldwide, Inc.

1100 NW Glisan Street, Suite 2B

Portland, OR 97209

(877) 769-9669

info@smww.com

http://www.smww.com

Sports Management Worldwide, Inc. is an agency that provides training programs for sports jobs, including that of sports agent. These programs can result in degrees and certifications. Sports Management Worldwide is a business that charges for courses and training. Its founder and president, Dr. G. Lynn Lashbrook, has been in sports management for more than 30 years, and represents more than 20 players in the National Football League. The agency's Web site includes information about becoming a sports agent.

SPORTSCASTER

American Sportscasters Association

225 Broadway, Suite 2030

New York, NY 10007

(212) 227-8080
lschwa8918@aol.com
http://www.americansportscasters.com

The American Sportscasters Association (ASA) was founded in 1980 to support, enhance, and promote the work of its members. Members include sportscasters, those interested in becoming sportscasters, and students. Information and guidance is available for aspiring sportscasters. The organization is known for its hall of fame, formerly housed in the MCI National Sports Gallery in Washington, D.C. The hall of fame had to be moved due to space constraints and the ASA is looking to have it placed elsewhere. The ASA holds an annual hall of fame awards dinner, at which time it recognizes the accomplishments of outstanding members.

SPORTS INFORMATION DIRECTOR

College Sports Information Directors of America
info@cosida.com
http://www.cosida.com

The College Sports Information Directors of America is an online organization of sports information directors from colleges across the country. Its Web site contains numerous links to a great variety of sports-related Web sites. There is a jobs center and useful information on topics relating to sports information.

SPORTS MASCOT

MascotNet
http://www.mascot.net

Since 1995, MascotNet has provided non-commercial information and share technology for the world's greatest costumed characters.

SPORTS PHOTOGRAPHER

SportsShooter.com
PO Box 5124
Pleasanton, CA 94566
sportsshooter@sportsshooter.com

http://www.sportshooter.comThis online association is invaluable for anyone who is a sports photographer, or who aspires to be one. The Web site includes information on how to get started in sports photography, shooting tips from photographers who have been working for a long time, contact information for photographers, online discussion groups, and much more. There also is a members-only site, which entitles you to be listed in the directory, display some of your work, and other benefits. The organization, started in 1998 as an online newsletter by a sports photographer for USA Today, has more than 7,000 members. You must be 18 to be a member. The site, however, is packed with great information for non-members, as well.

SPORTS PSYCHOLOGIST

American Psychological Association: Exercise and Sport Psychology
750 First Street, NE
Washington, DC 20002-4242
(800) 374-2721
division@apa.org
http://www.apa.org

The American Psychological Association's Exercise and Sports Psychology division was founded in 1986 to further the foundations of sport psychology, which at that time was a fairly new field. Today, this division of the American Psychological Association has more than 1,000 members as the field of sport psychology continues to expand.

The division provides an opportunity for scientists and practitioners to communicate and work together on projects concerning sport injury and rehabilitation, counseling of athletes, determining talent of athletes, youth sports, and other topics. The division's Web site, which is maintained by the University of North Texas Center for Sports Psychology, includes career information for those interested in becoming a sports psychologist.

SPORTSWRITER

Institute for International Sport
The Feinstein Building, University of
  Rhode Island
3045 Kingstown Road
PO Pox 1710
Kingston, RI 02881
(401) 874-2375
iis@internationalsport.com
http://www.internationalsport.com

The Institute for International Sport (IIS) was founded in 1986 by Daniel E. Doyle, Jr., a Trinity College basketball coach who wanted to promote sports as a means of advancing international friendships and relationships. The IIS promotes sportsmanship and education in sports, and sponsors events such as national sportsmanship day and a center for sports parenting. One of the IIS's premier events is the ethics and the sports media conference. There are links on the IIS Web site that provide more information about the conferernce.

STADIUM VENDOR

National Association of Concessionaires
35 East Wacker Drive
Suite 1816
Chicago, IL 60601

info@NAConline.org
http://NAConline.org
(312) 236-3858

NAC is a trade association for the recreation and leisure-time food and beverage concessions industry. It provides a highly diversified membership with information and services aimed at enhancing standards of quality and professionalism throughout the industry. NAC offers insurance policies for members that cover such areas as property, liability, and employee benefits. The association holds an annual convention, which features an educational conference on a wide range of topics and encourages interaction among those in the concessions industry. In conjunction with the trade show, NAC holds a trade show. The association twice a year publishes a newsletter and a magazine, Concession Profession.

TEAM PHYSICIAN

American College of Sports Medicine
401 West Michigan Street
Indianapolis, IN 46202-3233
(317) 637-9200
info@acsm.org
http://www.acsm.org

The American College of Sports Medicine (ACSM) is a professional organization with members that include doctors and others who have earned undergraduate, master's, or doctorate degrees from accredited schools in any area relating to health, exercise science, or physical education. People working in the area of health or physical education who have at least a bachelor's degree in another area also are eligible for membership, as are students. The ACSM offers a variety of member services including certification and credentialing opportunities, workshops, professional training, regional memberships, a newsletter, meetings and conferences, and grants incentives. The ACSM Web site contains general information on sports medicine, and provides a variety of links to other informative sites.

TENNIS PRO

United States Tennis Association
70 West Red Oak Lane
White Plains, NY 10604
(914) 696-7000
http://www.usta.com

The United States Tennis Association (USTA) was founded in 1881 to serve as the national governing body for the sport of tennis. It has worked since its inception to promote the growth of the sport at every level. The USTA, which is the largest tennis association in the world, is involved with tennis from the community level to the professional level, and holds the yearly US Open tennis tournament. The USTA Web site contains information about learning to play tennis, the lives of professional players, equipment, and more. It also provides information about joining the USTA, which provides benefits and opportunities, including the chance to play USTA league tennis.

TENNIS REFEREE

United States Tennis Association
70 West Red Oak Lane
White Plains, NY 10604
(914) 696-7000
http://www.usta.com

The United States Tennis Association (USTA) was founded in 1881 to serve as the national governing body for the sport of tennis. It has worked since its inception to promote the growth of the sport at every level. The USTA, which is the largest tennis association in the world, is involved with tennis from the community level to the professional level, and holds the yearly US Open tennis tournament. It also certifies officials at all levels of tennis, and oversees the process of placing officials at various events. The Web site provides a directory of tennis referees, information about training opportunities, and reading recommendations for referees.

ZAMBONI DRIVER

Zamboni Merchandising Company, Inc.
PO Box 1248
Paramount, CA 90723
(562) 663-1650
info@zamboni.com
http://www.zamboni.com

The Zamboni Merchandising Company was founded in 1950 by inventor Frank J. Zamboni, the man who invented the original ice resurfacing machine. In 2001 the company created the Frank J. Zamboni award to honor outstanding and innovative contributions to the ice skating industry. The company's Web site explains how the machines work and lists the different models available, has a special section for kids and students, and has lots of interesting facts about ice resurfacing and the machines used.

APPENDIX B. ONLINE CAREER RESOURCES

This volume offers a look inside a wide range of unusual and unique careers that might appeal to someone interested in jobs in the sports field. While it highlights general information, it's really only a quick snapshot of this very large field. The entries are intended to merely whet your appetite, and provide you with some career options you may never have known existed.

Before jumping into any career, you'll want to do more research to make sure that it's really something you want to pursue. You'll most likely want to learn as much as you can about the careers in which you are interested. That way, as you continue to research and talk to people in those particular fields, you can ask informed and intelligent questions that will help you make your decisions. You might want to research the education options for learning the skills you'll need to be successful, along with scholarships, work-study programs, and other opportunities to help you finance that education. And you might want answers to questions that weren't addressed in this book. If you search long enough, you can find just about anything using the Internet, including additional information about the jobs featured in this book.

✳ **A word about Internet safety:** The Internet is a wonderful resource for networking. Many job and career sites have forums where students can interact with other people interested in and working in that field. Some sites even offer online chats where people can communicate with each other in real time. They provide students and jobseekers opportunities to make connections and maybe even begin to lay the groundwork for future employment. But as you use these forums and chats, remember, anyone could be on the other side of that computer screen, telling you exactly what you want to hear. It's easy to get wrapped up in the excitement of the moment when you are on a forum or in a chat, interacting with people who share your career interests and aspirations. Be cautious about what kind of personal information you make available on the forums and in the chats; never give out your full name, address, or phone number. And never agree to meet with someone you have met online.

SEARCH ENGINES

When looking for information, there are lots of search engines that will help you to find out more about these jobs along with others that might interest you. While you might already have a favorite search engine, take some time to check out some of the others that are out there. Some have features that might help you find information you can't find elsewhere with the others. Several engines will offer suggestions for ways to narrow your results, or related phrases you might want to check out, along with your search results. This is handy if you are having trouble locating exactly what you want.

Another good thing to do is to learn how to use the advanced search features of your favorite search engines. Knowing that might help you to zero-in on exactly the information for which you are searching without wasting time looking through pages of irrelevant hits.

As you use the Internet to search information on the perfect career, keep in mind that like anything you find on the Internet, you need to consider the source from which the information comes.

Some of the most popular Internet search engines are:

AllSearchEngines.com
www.allsearchengines.com
This search engine index has links to the major search engines along with search engines grouped by topic. The site includes a page with more than 75 career and job search engines at http://www. allsearchengines.com/careerjobs.html.

AlltheWeb
http://www.alltheweb.com

AltaVista
http://www.altavista.com

Ask.com
http://www.ask.com

Dogpile
http://www.dogpile.com

Excite
http://www.excite.com

Google
http://www.google.com

HotBot
http://www.hotbot.com

LookSmart
http://www.looksmart.com

Lycos
http://www.lycos.com

Mamma.com
http://www.mamma.com

MSN Network
http://www.msn.com

My Way
http://www.goto.com

Teoma
http://www.directhit.com

Vivisimo
http://www.vivisimo.com

Yahoo!
http://www.yahoo.com

HELPFUL WEB SITES

The Internet is a wealth of information on careers—everything from the mundane to the outrageous. There are thousands of sites devoted to helping you find the perfect job for you; your interests, skills, and talents. The sites listed here are some of the most helpful ones that the authors came across and/or used while researching the jobs in this volume. The sites are listed in alphabetical order. They are offered for your information, and are not endorsed by the authors.

All Experts
http://www.allexperts.com
"The oldest & largest free Q&A service on the Internet," AllExperts.com has thousands of volunteer experts to answer your questions. You can also read replies to questions asked by other people. Each expert has an online profile to help you pick someone who might be best suited to answer your question. Very easy to use, it's a great resource for finding

experts who can help to answer your questions.

America's Career InfoNet
http://www.acinet.org

A wealth of information! You can get a feel for the general job market; check out wages and trends in a particular state for different jobs; and learn more about the knowledge, skills, abilities, and tasks for specific careers; and learn about required certifications and how to get them. You can search over 5,000 scholarship and other financial opportunities to help you further your education. A huge career resources library has links to nearly 6,500 online resources. And for fun, you can take a break and watch one of nearly 450 videos featuring real people at work; everything from custom tailors to engravers, glassblowers to silversmiths.

Backdoor Jobs: Short-Term Job Adventures, Summer Jobs, Volunteer Vacations, Work Abroad, and More
http://www.backdoorjobs.com

This is the Web site of the popular book by the same name, now in its third edition. While not as extensive as the book, the site still offers a wealth of information for people looking for short-term opportunities: internships, seasonal jobs, volunteer vacations, and work abroad situations. Job opportunities are classified into several categories: Adventure Jobs, Camps, Ranches & Resort Jobs, Ski Resort Jobs, Jobs in the Great Outdoors, Nature Lover Jobs, Sustainable Living and Farming Work, Artistic & Learning Adventures, Heart Work, and Opportunities Abroad.

Boston Works—Job Explainer
http://bostonworks.boston.com/globe/
job_explainer/archive.html

For nearly 18 months, the Boston Globe *ran a weekly series profiling a wide range of careers. Some of the jobs were more traditional. Others were very unique and unusual. The profiles discuss an "average" day, challenges of the job, required training, salary, and more. Each profile gives an up-close, personal look at that particular career. In addition, The Boston Works Web site (http://bostonworks.boston.com) has a lot of good, general employment-related information.*

Career Planning at About.com
http://careerplanning.about.com

Like most of the other About.com topics, the career planning area is a wealth of information, and links to other information on the Web. Among the excellent essentials are career planning A-to-Z, a career planning glossary, information on career choices, and a free career planning class. There are many great articles and other excellent resources.

Career Prospects in Virginia
http://www3.ccps.virginia.edu/career_
prospects/default-search.html

Career Prospects is a database of entries with information about over 400 careers. Developed by the Virginia Career Resource Network, the online career information resource of the Virginia Department of Education, Office of Career and Technical Education Services, was intended as a source of information about jobs "important to Virginia," but is actually a great source of information for anyone. While some of the information such as wages, outlook, and some of the requirements may apply only to Virginia, other information for each job, such as what it's like, getting ahead, skills, and links, will be of help to anyone interested in that career.

Career Voyages

http://www.careervoyages.gov

"The ultimate road trip to career success," sponsored by the U.S. Department of Labor and the U.S. Department of Education. This site features sections for students, parents, career changers, and career advisors with information and resources aimed to that specific group. The FAQ offers great information about getting started, the high-growth industries, how to find your perfect job, how to make sure you're qualified for the job you want, tips for paying for the training and education you need, and more. Also interesting are the hot careers and the emerging fields.

Dream Jobs

http://www.salary.com/careers/ layouthtmls/crel_display_Cat10.html

The staff at Salary.com takes a look at some wild, wacky, outrageous, and totally cool ways to earn a living. The jobs they highlight include pro skateboarder, computer game guru, nose, diplomat, and much more. The profiles don't offer links or resources for more information, but they are informative and fun to read.

ESPN Jobs

http://www.joinourteam.espn.com/ joinourteam/

ESPN's mission is to attract and retain the most talented people by fostering an environment for them to thrive in their work efforts. Use the search criteria below to view a list of ESPN job openings and to apply online. To ensure you view all opportunities, select the "select all" in the location field. If you don't find a current opening, you can set up a job search agent or submit a resume to be considered when an opportunity becomes available.

Find It! in DOL

http://www.dol.gov/dol/findit.htm

A handy source for finding information at the extensive U.S. Department of Labor Web site. You can "Find It!" by broad topic category, or by audience, which includes a section for students.

Fine Living: *Radical Sabbatical*

http://www.fineliving.com/fine/episode_ archive/0,1663,FINE_1413_14,00. html#Series873

The show Radical Sabbatical *on the Fine Living network looks at people willing to take a chance and follow their dreams and passions. The show focuses on individuals between the ages of 20 and 65 who have made the decision to leave successful, lucrative careers to start over, usually in an unconventional career. You can read all about these people and their journeys on the show's Web site.*

Free Salary Survey Reports and Cost of Living Reports

http://www.salaryexpert.com

Based on information from a number of sources, Salary Expert will tell you what kind of salary you can expect to make for a certain job in a certain geographic location. Salary Expert has information on hundreds of jobs; everything from your more traditional white- and blue-collar jobs, to some unique and out of the ordinary professions like acupressurist, blacksmith, denture waxer, taxidermist, and many others. With sections covering schools, crime, community comparison, community explorer, and more, the moving center is a useful area for people who need to relocate for training or employment.

Fun Jobs

http://www.funjobs.com

Fun Jobs has job listings for adventure, outdoor, and fun jobs at ranches, camps, ski resorts, and more. The job postings have a lot of information about the position, requirements, benefits, and responsibilities so that you know what you are getting into ahead of time. And, you can apply online for most of the positions. The Fun Companies link will let you look up companies in an A-to-Z listing, or you can search for companies in a specific area or by keyword. The company listings offer you more detailed information about the location, types of jobs available, employment qualifications, and more.

Girls Can Do

http://www.girlscando.com

"Helping Girls Discover Their Life's Passions," Girls Can Do has opportunities, resources, and a lot of other cool stuff for girls ages 8 to 18. Girls can explore sections on Outdoor Adventure, Sports, My Body, The Arts, Sci-Tech, Change the World, and Learn, Earn, and Intern. In addition to reading about women in all sorts of careers, girls can explore a wide range of opportunities and information that will help them grow into strong, intelligent, capable women.

Great Web Sites for Kids

http://www.ala.org/gwstemplate.cfm?section=greatwebsites&template=/cfapps/gws/default.cfm

Great Web Sites for Kids is a collection of more than 700 sites organized into a variety of categories, including animals, sciences, the arts, reference, social sciences, and more. All of the sites included here have been approved by a committee made up of professional librarians and educators. You can even submit your favorite great site for possible inclusion.

Hot Jobs: Career Tools

http://www.hotjobs.com/htdocs/tools/index-us.html

While the jobs listed at Hot Jobs are more on the traditional side, the Career Tools area has a lot of great resources for anyone looking for a job. You'll find information about how to write a resume and a cover letter, how to put together a career portfolio, interviewing tips, links to career assessments, and much more.

Job Descriptions & Job Details

http://www.job-descriptions.org

Search for descriptions and details for more than 13,000 jobs at this site. You can search for jobs by category or by industry. You'd probably be hard pressed to find a job that isn't listed here, and you'll probably find lots of jobs you never imagined existed. The descriptions and details are short, but it's interesting and fun, and might lead you to the career of your dreams.

Job Hunter's Bible

http://www.jobhuntersbible.com

This site is the official online supplement to the book What Color Is Your Parachute? A Practical Manual for Job-Hunters and Career-Changers, *and is a great source of information with lots of informative, helpful articles and links to many more resources.*

Job Profiles

http://www.jobprofiles.org

A collection of profiles where Experienced workers share about rewards of their job; stressful parts of the job; basic skills the job demands;

challenges of the future; and advice on entering the field. The careers include everything from baseball ticket manager to pastry chef and much, much more. The hundreds of profiles are arranged by broad category. While most of the profiles are easy to read, you can check out the How to Browse JobProfiles. org section (http://www.jobprofiles.org/ jphowto.htm) if you have any problems.

JobsInSports.Com
http://www.jobsinsports.com/subscribe.cfm

This Internet-based employment service is dedicated to helping you find a sports job, packed with job databases listing hundreds of jobs in the areas of sports marketing, sports media, sales, health & fitness, computers and high-tech, and administration/management. There's also an internship center specifically listing sports internships available for job seekers looking to gain experience, a sports contacts area with names and contact information for all of the major sports franchises, and a resume posting area where you can list your own resume.

Major Job Web sites at Careers.org
http://www.careers.org/topic/01_jobs_10.html

This page at the careers.org Web site has links for more than 40 of the Web's major job-related Web sites. While you're there, check out the numerous links to additional information.

Monster.com
http://www.monster.com

Monster.com is one of the largest and probably best known, job resource sites on the Web. It's really one-stop shopping for almost anything job-related that you can imagine. You can find a new job, network, update your resume, improve your skills, plan a job change or relocation, and so much more. Of special interest are the Monster: Cool Careers (http://change. monster.com/archives/coolcareers) and the Monster: Job Profiles (http://jobprofiles. monster.com) where you can read about some really neat careers. The short profiles also include links to additional information. The Monster: Career Advice section (http://content.monster.com/) has resume and interviewing advice, message boards where you can network, relocation tools and advice, and more.

Occupational Outlook Handbook
http://www.bls.gov/oco

Published by the U.S. Department of Labor, Bureau of Labor Statistics, the Occupational Outlook Handbook (sometimes referred to as the OOH) is the premiere source of career information. The book is updated every two years, so you can be assured that the information you are using to help make your decisions is current. The online version is very easy to use; you can search for a specific occupation, browse through a group of related occupations, or look through an alphabetical listing of all the jobs included in the volume. Each of the entries will highlight the general nature of the job, working conditions, training and other qualifications, job outlook, average earning, related occupations, and sources of additional information. Each entry covers several pages and is a terrific source to get some great information about a huge variety of jobs.

Online Sports.com Career Center
http://www.onlinesports.com/pages/CareerCenter.html

The Online Sports Career Center is a resource of sports-related career opportunities and a resume bank for potential employers within the many segments of the sports and recreation industries.

Online Sports.com: Sports Career Planning

http://www.onlinesports.com/sportstrust/

This page features two sports career-planning newsletters: Sports News *and* The Creative Athlete.

The Riley Guide: Employment Opportunities and Job Resources on the Internet

http://www.rileyguide.com

The Riley Guide is an amazing collection of job and career resources. Unless you are looking for something specific, one of the best ways to maneuver around the site is with the A-to-Z Index. You can find everything from links to careers in enology to information about researching companies and employers. The Riley Guide is a great place to find just about anything you might be looking for, and probably lots of things you aren't looking for. Be forewarned, it's easy to get lost in the A-to-Z Index, reading about all sorts of interesting things.

USA TODAY Career Focus

http://www.usatoday.com/careers/dream/dreamarc.htm

Several years ago, USA TODAY ran a series featuring people working in their dream jobs. In the profiles, people discuss how they got their dream job, what they enjoy the most about it, an average day, their education backgrounds, sacrifices they had to make for their jobs, and more. They also share words of advice for anyone hoping to follow in their footsteps. Most of the articles also feature links where you can find more information. The USATODAY.

com Job Center (http://www.usatoday.com/money/jobcenter/front.htm) also has links to lots of resources and additional information.

Women Sports Jobs

http://www.womensportsjobs.com/default.htm

This Web site is designed to help women find jobs in sports—sales, marketing, broadcasting, PR, coaching, officiating, health/fitness, athletic administration, event management, journalism, sporting goods, and more. The database is divided by industry categories, including: Professional Teams, College Athletics, Sporting Goods, Broadcast & Media, Sports Events, Recreation, Professional Services, Sports Associations, Sports Venues, Sports Technology/Internet, and High School Sports.

CAREER TESTS & INVENTORIES

If you have no idea what career is right for you, there are many resources available online that will help assess your interests and maybe steer you in the right direction. While some of the assessments charge a fee, there are many out there that are free. You can locate more tests and inventories by searching for "career tests," "career inventories," or "personality inventories." Some of the most popular assessments available online are:

Campbell Interest and Skill Survey (CISS)

http://www.usnews.com/usnews/edu/careers/ccciss.htm

Career Explorer

http://careerexplorer.net/aptitude.asp

Career Focus 2000 Interest Inventory

http://www.iccweb.com/careerfocus

The Career Interests Game
http://career.missouri.edu/students/
explore/careerinterestsgame.php

The Career Key
http://www.careerkey.org

CAREERLINK Inventory
http://www.mpc.edu/cl/cl.htm

Career Maze
http://www.careermaze.com/home.
asp?licensee=CareerMaze

Career Tests at CareerPlanner.com
http://www.careerplanner.com

FOCUS
http://www.focuscareer.com

Keirsey Temperament Test
http://www.keirsey.com

**Motivational Appraisal of Personal
Potential (MAPP)**
http://www.assessment.com

Myers-Briggs Personality Type
http://www.personalitypathways.com/
type_inventory.html

Princeton Review Career Quiz
http://www.princetonreview.com/cte/
quiz/default.asp

Skills Profiler
http://www.acinet.org/acinet/skills_home.
asp

READ MORE ABOUT IT

GENERAL

Culbreath, Alice N., and Saundra K. Neal. *Testing the Waters: A Teen's Guide to Career Exploration*. New York: JRC Consulting, 1999.

Farr, Michael, LaVerne L. Ludden, and Laurence Shatkin. *200 Best Jobs for College Graduates*. Indianapolis, Ind.: Jist Publishing, 2003.

Field, Shelly. *Career Opportunities in the Sports Industry*. New York: Checkmark Books, 2004.

Fischer, David. *The 50 Coolest Jobs in Sports*. New York: Macmillan Reference, 1997.

Fogg, Neeta, and Paul Harrington, Thomas Harrington. *College Majors Handbook with Real Career Paths and Payoffs: The Actual Jobs, Earnings, and Trends for Graduates of 60 College Majors*. Indianapolis, Ind.: Jist Publishing, 2004.

Giebel, Nancy. *Great Jobs for Physical Education Majors*. New York: McGraw-Hill, 2004.

Krannich, Ronald L., and Caryl Rae Krannich. *The Best Jobs for the 1990s and into the 21st Century*. Manassas Park, Va.: Impact Publications, 1995.

Mannion, James. *The Everything Alternative Careers Book: Leave the Office Behind and Embark on a New Adventure*. Boston: Adams, 2004.

McKinney, Anne. *Real Resumes for Sports Industry Jobs: including real resumes used to change careers and transfer skills to other industries*. New York: Prep Publishing, 2004.

U.S. Bureau of Labor Statistics. *Occupational Outlook Handbook, 2006-07*. Available online at http://stats.bls.gov/oco/home.htm

ATHLETIC DIRECTOR, HIGH SCHOOL

Koehler, Mike, and Nancy Giebel. *Athletic Director's Survival Guide*. Upper Saddle River, N.J.: Prentice Hall, 1997.

Mamchak, P., Susan, and Steven R. Mamchak. *Complete Communications Manual for Coaches and Athletic Directors*. Grand Rapids, Mich.: Parker Publishing Co., 1989.

BOXER

Halbert, Christy. *The Ultimate Boxer: Understanding the Sport and Skills of Boxing*. Brentwood, Tenn.: Impact Seminars, 2003.

Werner, Doug. *Boxer's Start-Up Guide: A Beginner's Guide to Boxing*. Chula Vista, Calif.: Tracks Publishing, 1998.

BOXING TRAINER

Scott, Danna. *Boxing: The Complete Guide to Training and Fitness*. New York: Perigee Trade, 2000.

Werner, Doug, and Mark Hatmaker. *Boxing Mastery: Advanced Technique, Tactics, and Strategies from the Sweet Science*. Chula Vista, Calif.: Tracks Publishing, 2004.

DRAG RACER

Genat, Robert. *American Drag Racer*. Osceola, Wisc.: Motorbooks International, 2001.

National Hot Rod Association. *The Fast Lane: The History of NHRA Drag Racing*. New York: Regan Books, 2001.

GOLF BALL DIVER

Coleman, Clay. *The Certified Diver's Handbook: The Complete Guide to Your Own Underwater Adventures.* Camden, Maine: International Marine/Rugged Mountain Press, 2004.

Graver, Dennis K. *Scuba Diving.* Champaign, Ill.: Human Kinetics Publishers, 2003.

GOLF CADDIE

Carrick, Michael, and Steve Duno. *Caddie Sense: Revelations of a PGA Tour Caddie on Playing the Game of Golf.* New York: Thomas Dunne Books, 2000.

Mackenzie, Richard. *A Wee Nip at the 19th Hole: A History of the St. Andrews Caddie.* Farmington, Mich.: Thompson Gale, 1997.

GOLF COURSE ARCHITECT

Doak, Tom, and Ben Crenshaw. *The Anatomy of a Golf Course: The Art of Architecture.* Springfield, N.J.: Burford Books, 1999.

Hurdzan, Michael J. *Golf Course Architecture: Design, Construction & Restoration.* Hoboken, N.J.: John Wiley & Sons, 1996.

GOLF PRO

McLean, Jim. *Golf Digest's Ultimate Drill Book.* New York: Gotham Books, 2003.

Newell, Steve and Sharon Lucas. *The Golf Instruction Manual.* London: DK Adult, 2001.

GOLF TOURNAMENT DIRECTOR

Feinstein, John. *Open: Inside the Ropes at Bethpage Black.* Boston: Back Bay Books, 2004.

Strege, John. *Tournament Week: Inside the Ropes and Behind the Scenes on the PGA Tour.* New York: HarperCollins Publishers, 2000.

GRAND PRIX DRESSAGE RIDER

Klimke, Reiner. *Klimke on Dressage: From the Young Horse Through Grand Prix.* Boonsboro, Md.: Half Halt Press, 1992.

Moon, Vicky. *Sunday Horse: Inside The Grand Prix Show Jumping Circuit.* Herndon, Va.: Capital Books, 2006.

Allen, Linda, and Dianna Robin Dennis. *101 Jumping Exercises for Horse & Rider.* North Adams, Mass.: Storey Publishing, 2002.

HOCKEY PLAYER

Smith, Michael A. *The Hockey Play Book: Teaching Hockey Systems.* Tonawanda, N.Y.: Firefly Books Ltd., 2005.

Twist, Peter. *Complete Conditioning for Ice Hockey.* Champaign, Ill.: Human Kinetics Press, 1996.

MINOR LEAGUE GENERAL MANAGER

Bess, Phillip. *City Baseball Magic—Plain Talk and Uncommon Sense About Cities and Baseball Parks.* St. Paul, Minn.: Knothole Press, 1999.

Johnson, Arthur T. *Minor League Baseball and Local Economic Development.* Champaign, Ill.: University of Illinois Press, 1995.

PERSONAL FITNESS TRAINER

Starkey, Lauren. *Certified Fitness Trainer Career Starter.* New York: LearningExpress, 2002.

Thornton, Ed. *It's More Than Just Making Them Sweat: A Career Training Guide for Personal Fitness Trainers.* Bandon, Ore.: Robert D. Reed Publishers, 2001.

PIT CREW MEMBER

McReynolds, Larry, and Bob Zeller. *The Big Picture: My Life From Pit Road to the Broadcast Booth.* Phoenix: David Bull Publishing, 2002.

Schaefer, A.R. *Racing With The Pit Crew.* London: Capstone Press, 2005.

RACEHORSE GROOM

Eng, Richard. *Betting on Horse Racing For Dummies.* Chicago: For Dummies, 2005.

Reynolds, Sue. *The Complete Guide to Horse Careers.* Livermore, Colo.: New Horizons Equine Educational Center, 1998.

SCOREBOARD OPERATOR

Schwarz, Alan. *The Numbers Game: Baseball's Lifelong Fascination with Statistics.* New York: St. Martins Press, 2004.

James, Bill. *The New Bill James Historical Baseball Abstract.* New York: Simon & Schuster, 2001.

SNOWBOARD INSTRUCTOR

Goldman, Greg. *Snowboarding: The Essential Guide to Equipment and Technique.* London: New Holland Publishers, 2001.

Ryan, Kevin. *The Illustrated Guide to Snowboarding.* Columbus, Ohio: McGraw-Hill, 1998.

SPORTS AGENT

Shropshire, Kenneth L., and Timothy Davis. *The Business of Sports Agents.* Philadelphia: University of Pennsylvania Press, 2002.

Yaeger, Don, and Drew Rosenhaus. *A Shark Never Sleeps: Wheeling and Dealing With the NFL's Most Ruthless Agent.* New York: Atria, 1998.

SPORTSCASTER

Hedrick, Tom. *The Art of Sportscasting: How to Build a Successful Career.* South Bend, Ind.: Diamond Communications, 2000.

Schultz, Bradley. *Sports Broadcasting.* Burlington, Mass.: Focal Press, 2001.

SPORTS INFORMATION DIRECTOR

Helitzer, Melvin. *The Dream Job: Sports Publicity, Promotion and Marketing.* Athens, Ohio: University Sports Press, 1999.

Nichols, William, Patrick Moynahan, Allan Hall, and Janis Taylor. *Media Relations in Sport.* Morgantown, W. Va.: Fitness Information Technology, 2001.

SPORTS MASCOT

Riggs, Adam. *Critter Costuming: Making Mascots and Fabricating Fursuits.* New York: Ibexa Press, 2004.

Fournier, Peter J. *The Handbook of Mascots and Nicknames.* New York: Raja and Assoc., 2004.

SPORTS PHOTOGRAPHER

Arndt, David Neil. *How to Shoot and Sell Sports Photography.* Buffalo, N.Y.: Amherst Media, 1999.

Timacheff, Serge, and David Karlins. *Digital Sports Photography: Take Winning Shots Every Time.* Hoboken, N.J.: John Wiley& Sons, 2005.

SPORTS PSYCHOLOGIST

Murphy, Shane. *The Sport Psych Handbook.* Champaign, Ill.: Human Kinetic Publishers, 2004.

Weinberg, Robert S., and Daniel Gould. *Foundations of Sport and Exercise Psychology*. Champaign, Ill.: Human Kinetic Publishers, 1999.

SPORTSWRITER
Craig, Steve. *Sportswriting: A Beginner's Guide*. Shoreham, Vt.: Discover Writing Press, 2002.
Kovach, Bill, and Tom Rosenstiel. The *Elements of Journalism: What Newspeople Should Know and The Public Should Expect*. New York: Three Rivers Press, 2001.

STADIUM VENDOR
Smith, Curt. *Storied Stadiums: Baseball's History Through Its Ballparks*. New York: Carroll & Graf Publishers, 2001.
Solveig Paulson, Russell. *Peanuts, Popcorn, Ice Cream, Candy and Soda Pop and How They Began*. Nashville, Tenn.: Abingdon Press, 1970.

TEAM PHYSICIAN
Birrer, Richard B., and Francis G. O'Connor. *Sports Medicine for the Primary Care Physician*. Boca Raton, Fla.: CRC Press, 2004.

O'Connor, Francis G. *Sports Medicine: Just the Facts*. Columbus, Ohio: McGraw-Hill, 2004.

TENNIS PRO
Sadzeck, Tom. *Tennis Skills: The Player's Guide*. Tonawanda, N.Y.: Firefly Books, 2001.
Yandell, John. *Visual Tennis*. Champaign, Ill.: Human Kinetics Publishers, 1999.

TENNIS REFEREE
Lindsey, Crawford, and Rod Cross. *Technical Tennis: Racquets, Strings, Balls, Courts, Spin, Bounce*. Vista, Calif.: United States Racquet Stringers Association, 2005.
United States Tennis Association. *Official Rules of Tennis*. Chicago, Ill.: Triumph Books, 2004.

ZAMBONI DRIVER
Andreen, Jan, Merv Magus, and Barbara Sommons. *Zamboni is Not a Dessert*. Philadelphia: Xlibris Corporation, 2001.
Cohen, Jason. *Zamboni Rodeo: Chasing Hockey Dreams from Austin to Albuquerque*. Vancouver, British Columbia: Greystone Books, 2003.

INDEX

Page numbers in **bold** indicate major treatment of a topic.